WITHDRAWN

WILLIAM INGE

GARLAND REFERENCE LIBRARY
OF THE HUMANITIES
(VOL. 235)

The best g all
birthdays
to
mom —

Bill

Courtesy of The William Inge Collection,
Independence Community College, Independence, Kansas

WILLIAM INGE
A Bibliography

Arthur F. McClure

GARLAND PUBLISHING, INC. • NEW YORK & LONDON
1982

Library of Congress Cataloging in Publication Data

McClure, Arthur F.
  William Inge: a bibliography.

  (Garland reference library of the humanities ;
v. 235)
  Includes index.
  1. Inge, William—Bibliography. I. Title. II. Series.
Z8437.5.M38 [PS3517.N265]   016.812'54   80-8500
ISBN 0-8240-9486-7   AACR2

Printed on acid-free, 250-year-life paper
Manufactured in the United States of America

This volume is dedicated to MARTHA CABLE WAGNER and RUTH HERNDON ROULUND whose "sweetness of character" as young Kansas schoolteachers provided such a lasting gift to at least one of their former fourth grade students.

Report on Niger Mission, 208–10, 220; consulted by Hill, 228–9; joins *Ogboni*, 270

Wood Report, 208–10, 220

World War, First, 151, 303, 324, 331, 341–2

Worship: Nigerian forms of, 243, 270; Christian, in schools, 292; alien forms in African Churches, 343

Wright, H., 196

Yola, 125

Yonkers, 255

Yoruba, Yorubaland:

Politics and society: situation on arrival of missionaries, 5–6; *Akus*, 7, 212; position of Ẹgba in, 6; slave trade in, 7; geographical factors, 10; British aid to, 10, 13; interstate warfare, 10, 338; unity of, 11; attitude to British government, 13, 15–16; pacification of, 29–69, 267; British occupation of, 29, 33, 38, 42–4, 54–5; instability in 1889, 32; French influence, 33; Sixteen Years' war, 33–5, 38–9, 56, 338; Alafin of Ọyọ titular head, 38–9; French designs on, 50–3; and Sokoto caliphate, 117; Ọni of Ifẹ spiritual head, 155; and indirect rule, 173; nationalists' outlook, 194; Ethiopianism 194–6; customs, 245, 257–8, 264–5; names, 258–9; origins of, 260; religious state, 260–1; mythology and religion, 264–5; West African Psychical Research Institute, 264; title system, 266; and *Ogboni*, 267; rubber and indigo, 289; chiefs' prestige falls, 289; government education, 300; slavery in, 331–3; labour requisition in, 339

Language and literature: 40, 52, 277, 283

Missionary activity: arrival of missionaries, 5–6; their influence, 5–6, 8; 29–32; and Bishop Crowther, 16;

position of missionaries in interior, 30, 71; S.M.A. in, 33; African missionaries in, 38; link with Lagos Government, 39, 43–4; J. B. Wood, 39–40; proposed episcopate, 40, 189, 196, 225, 228; in diocese of Sierra Leone, 47; few converts in, 133; educated Yorubas, 145; response to missionary appeal, 155–6; Wesleyan missions, 156, 165–6; 213, strained relations with administrators, 161–3; attitude of European missionaries, 183; Yoruba Chruch, 188; churches in interior, 197, 201; Blyden's tour of, 219; Herbert Macaulay's Tour, 238; effect of Reformed Ogboni, 276–7; education in, 285; agents attracted to government jobs, 288; demand for village education, 290–1; school fees, 292; industrial education, 296–7; and liquor traffic, 307–10, 318, 327; response to Christianity, 343; Wesleyans 165–6; C.M.S., 196, 208, 292

Yoruba Country and its Tribes (J. O. George), 260

Yoruba Heathenism (James Johnson), 264

Yoruba History (Payne), 260

Yoruba Mythology (Lijadu), 264

Yoruba Research Scheme, 260

Yorubas, History of the, (Samuel Johnson), 260

Young, John *see* Eyamba V, King

Young Calabar movement, 26, 74–5, 86, 98

Zanzibar, Sultan of, 148

Zappa, Fr. 288

Zaria (map, p. 119), 122, 131–4, 138; Emir of, 133–4, 147, 149, 152; C.M.S. in, 140, 142, 150; Resident at, 143; baptism incident at, 148; oppression in, 152

Zinder, 135

Zinna (map, p. 119), 345

CONTENTS

II. Biographical Information

III. Critical Articles and Reviews of Inge's Work

IV. William Inge and Film

Contents   *ix*

PREFACE

This bibliography attempts to present a detailed picture of William Motter Inge's work as teacher, journalist, and author. The first part, devoted to his published writings, is, I hope, inclusive. The second part, devoted to opinions about Inge and his work, is necessarily selective. The critical work listed here should offer some evidence of the permanence of Inge's reputation as a writer.

Compiling a bibliography is one of the least appreciated scholarly activities. Many voices scoffingly dismiss the process as antiquarian, the product as a mere list with little value. But in fact the bibliographer imposes order and thus makes possible systematic exploration of many new areas of investigation into a body of literary work.

An Inge bibliography is long overdue. There has long been a need for a current and more complete bibliography representing the varying critical attitudes to Inge's work. The present book is an attempt in that direction. William Inge did not leave behind a large body of work, but he was a skilled writer who understood small town life and the lonely existence of some of its people. Many critics and literary historians are aware that the Midwest has been neglected in the American literary scene. It is the conviction of this compiler that research into and scholarship about Inge's career will continue. Accordingly, this bibliography attempts to present a thorough listing of Inge's work as well as to survey the salient features of the basic critical works about him.

It seems possible to reevaluate the customary estimate of Inge's literary reputation in light of the material presented in this book. Perhaps the most important purpose of this work is to suggest some new areas of critical and historical investigation into Inge's work. It is hoped that this volume will not only be of use in assisting ongoing research, but will also stimulate new research into Inge's life, works, and literary career.

Acknowledging assistance in a project of this sort seems an impossible task. Any completeness and value which this listing has could not have been achieved without the help, generosity, and kindness of many people. My interest in William Inge began at the University of Kansas under the patient and informed guidance of Professor Donald R. McCoy. My continued interest in a possible bibliographical work was enhanced in the earliest stages by my friend and colleague Glenn Q. Pierce, Professor of Theatre at Central Missouri State University. The initial expression of interest in the publication of this bibliography by Richard Newman of Garland has been most appreciated. The formidable typing and editorial tasks which the final version of the volume have demanded could not have been completed without the dedication and skill of Liz Snyder Rotert, friend and trusted associate. And thanks to my wife, Judy, and my children, Allison, Kyle, Amy, and Sam, for their warm and invaluable enthusiasm.

INTRODUCTION

William Motter Inge is the recognized dramatic chronicler of the Midwest. The plays which established Inge as a major American dramatist of his region were *Come Back, Little Sheba*, 1950; *Picnic*, 1953; *Bus Stop*, 1955; and *The Dark at the Top of the Stairs*, 1958. All four were Broadway successes and all four were subsequently made into motion pictures. For *Come Back, Little Sheba*, Inge won the George Jean Nathan Award and the Theatre Time Award. Shirley Booth later won an Academy Award for her performance in the film version. For *Picnic*, Inge won the Pulitzer Prize in Drama, the Outer Circle Award, and the New York Drama Critics Award, among others. In addition, Inge received an Academy Award in 1961 for his original screenplay, *Splendor in the Grass*. According to critic Robert Brustein, until William Inge, Broadway had treated the Midwest as a "large mass of unidentified land west of Sardi's restaurant and east of Schwab's drugstore" in Hollywood. Inge's best writing painted a much truer picture of many aspects of Midwestern life. His works demonstrated that the region offered more culturally than many patronizing observers had previously supposed. William Inge was a Midwesterner by birth. More precisely, he was a Kansan who became the first major American playwright to deal seriously with that region. So far he is the only one.

Inge was born 3 May 1913, in Independence, Kansas. He attended local schools and graduated with a B.A. from the University of Kansas in 1935. After a career as a teacher and a sometime drama critic, his first Broadway play, *Come Back, Little Sheba*, received mixed reviews, but ran for 190 performances, establishing Inge as a major American dramatist. It was set in "a Midwestern city." Thus began the theatrical geography that remained the source and setting of Inge's most successful works. It is interesting that late in his career when his personal and professional life fell on hard times, it was a shift away from the Midwest as a setting that accompanied his failing powers as a writer.

Any proposed study of the geography of William Inge must center around Inge's compassion for and understanding of the lives of small town people. The men and women he created in his works often lead despairing lives, but Inge's basic attitude toward them is fondness, rather than hatred or contempt. Certain values are accepted or rejected by his characters. The people in his works are ordinary human beings whose counterparts might be found anywhere—harassed parents, rebellious children, businessmen, frustrated schoolteachers, itinerant bums, and such. Nevertheless, the geographical background always appears to be somewhere between the Mississippi and the Rockies, out on the middle ground of the Great Plains, and it always seems that what is happening probably could not occur elsewhere, at least not in exactly the same way. Inge's strength is in the setting of his plays. He saw the Midwest as a great middle ground with little reference to *where* or *when* his characters lived but mostly *how* and *why*. Inge transcended region even though his plays have regional qualities. His plays are "provincial" with no "provincialism." And while his stories concern the "heartland" of America, they have meaning to all who are interested in sharing the visions and frustrations of ordinary men and women anywhere.

The real world of William Inge was the Midwest. *Picnic* is set in "a small Kansas town," and Inge refers to Cherryvale in southeastern Kansas as well as Kansas City in the play. *Bus Stop* is set in a "small town about thirty miles west of Kansas City." Cherie, the main character, is carefully described by Inge. "Her origin is the Ozarks and her speech is Southern." She sang in the "Blue Dragon" nightclub in the stockyards of Kansas City. In *Bus Stop* Inge also mentions the "Menniger Clinic" in Topeka as well as Joplin, Missouri, and "Kanz City," reflecting a local and regional pronunciation.

Small towns fascinated Inge. He felt that "people exist as individuals in small towns. Everybody knows everybody else's business, but not so in cities." His play *The Dark at the Top of the Stairs* is set in a "small Oklahoma town close to Oklahoma City" in the early 1920s.

Inge wrote of the power and beauty of Kansas so often overlooked by outsiders. *Picnic* is set against the colorful, sweeping vastness of Kansas skies and fields, of grain elevators and busy yards. It is the earthy story of a stranger in town, and the effect he has on the lives of its people, especially its women, during the twenty-four hours surrounding a Labor Day picnic. The town in the story is "Salinson," Kansas, a wordplay on the real towns of Hutchinson and Salina. Inge's strength as a depictor of the charm, naturalness, and compassion of the people of the Midwest was enhanced when much of the film version of *Picnic* was filmed on location in Kansas in the spring of 1955. The famous "picnic" sequence was filmed in Riverside Park in Halstead, Kansas. The film has since become something of a classic. It underscores beautifully Inge's intention of the Labor Day picnic as a symbol of the life of a small town. The film's Kansas location shooting helped also to reinforce the feeling for ordinary people that gives his works their human appeal. Other filming was done in Salina in its Union Pacific railroad yards and along the Smoky Hill River. The huge grain elevators in Hutchinson were also used in the film, and other scenes were shot in Nickerson and Sterling.

Inge wrote of the "sweetness of character" that the people of the Midwest possessed. *Picnic* is the Great American Dream set in Kansas with its overlooked beauty that some observers often joked about. Inge had great affection for his community, and his characters nearly always accept who they are. This makes his plays real rather than ideal. For Inge, the important thing in life was to find out *who* you are and live by your own lights, and not to pursue either social ideas of success and ambition or accept a morality laid down by the strong demands of authority. Inge tells us that we should accept our own nature and shape our lives from it.

In 1968, Inge wrote the Introduction to *The Plains States*, a Time-Life Library of America volume in a series that investigated the various regions of America. In the opening paragraph, Inge reveals some of his thoughts concerning the human geography of his native region.

> The Plains States are the heart of our nation, and that heart beats slow and sure year after year while the cities on the coastlines, crowded, competitively industrial, cosmopo-

lite and more seemingly vulnerable to foreign influences as
well as attacks in times of war, manifest our nation's violent
anxieties and antagonisms. Nowhere can we find a closer
correlation of landscape and character than in the Plains
States. The people there are, for the most part, as plain and
level and unadorned as the scenery. New fashions, new in-
ventions seldom emanate from this region, and its native
artists usually go to some other part of the country to find
appreciation and encouragement. In recent years at least,
one has seldom heard of riots, strikes or demonstrations in
Kansas, Missouri, Nebraska, Iowa, Minnesota and the
Dakotas.

It should be noticed that Inge avoids the use of the word
"flat." He goes on to write that:

> Not all the land in the Plains States is level. Much of it is
> gently rolling, and there are a few mountains. But those
> areas are exceptions in this level land. Level, but not flat.
> When we speak of anything as *flat* we imply that it holds no
> content of interest. But we use the word *level* as synony-
> mous with honesty and truth.
>
> Instinctively, I call the land *level*. People who do not
> appreciate this region call it *flat*. And perhaps one has to be
> born and raised in the Plains States to see and feel their
> serene and understated beauty. People from the East are
> slow to respond to it, if at all. And they deplore its lack of
> Eastern culture.

It might be said that the world of William Inge was that of
the lingering heart. His work depicts people who either have
once known joy, or wonder why they have never experienced it.
Personally, Inge was a very sad man. The old joys and the old
simplicities of life were what his genius addressed itself to—but
his lingering heart ultimately could not cope with life as he knew
it near the end. Although his work had once received critical
praise, he fell from favor and was criticized as out of date and
sentimental. Perhaps Inge's most human quality was displayed
by his investigation of the typical behavior of seemingly conven-
tional characters and their reconciliation to and acceptance of
what cannot be changed. Inge wrote, "Maybe we find beauty
only in what we know. Mountains have never intrigued me.

They have none of the mystery of the prairie, where one can always feel close to some eternal truth concerning man and his place in the universe." That mystery and that truth became the core of his literary geography. We are all richer for it.

CHRONOLOGY

1913   Born in Independence, Kansas, 3 May, the fifth and last child of Maude Sarah Gibson and Luther Clayton Inge. As a child, Inge made several trips to Kansas City to see plays.

1927–30   Attended Independence High School, Independence. As a high school student Inge attended a Kansas City performance by Katharine Cornell in *The Barretts of Wimpole Street* and was greatly impressed.

1930–35   Attended the University of Kansas. Inge was a member of Sigma Nu fraternity along with Clarence Kelly, later to be Director of the FBI. Inge received the B.A. degree on 10 June 1935, just past his 22nd birthday.

1932   Acted in a Toby tent show during the summer.

1933   Worked with the summer theater sponsored by the Culver Military Academy.

1934   Actor with Maxinuckee Mummers during the summer.

1935–36   Attended George Peabody College of Teachers, but because of illness, left two weeks before graduation.

1936   Worked during the summer on a road gang for the Kansas State Highway Department.

1936–37   News announcer for radio station KFH, Wichita.

1937–38   English teacher in Cherokee County Community High School, Columbus, Kansas.

1938   Completed work for M.A. in English during the summer and was awarded degree.

1938–43   Taught English composition and drama at Stephens College, Columbia, Missouri. Famed actress Maude Adams headed drama department.

1943–46   Employed as art, music, book, and drama critic for the *St. Louis Star-Times*.

1944   Interviewed Tennessee Williams for newspaper in November (interview published 11 November). Inge traveled to Chicago to see *The Glass Menagerie*.

1945   Wrote his first play, *Farther Off from Heaven*.

1946–49   Taught English at Washington University, St. Louis.

1947   *Farther Off from Heaven* produced by Margo Jones's Little Theatre Group in Dallas.

1949   *Come Back, Little Sheba* given a tryout by the Theatre Guild in Westport, Connecticut, opening on 4 September.

1950   *Come Back, Little Sheba* produced on Broadway. Inge moves to New York after a two-month residence in southern Connecticut. Inge undergoes psychoanalysis a few weeks after the opening of the play. In the summer he begins work on a new play, *Picnic*.

1953   *Picnic* produced on Broadway; movie rights sold for $300,000. Wins the Pulitzer Prize. Joins Alcoholics Anonymous.

1955   *Bus Stop* produced on Broadway.

1957   *The Dark at the Top of the Stairs* produced on Broadway.

1959   *A Loss of Roses* produced on Broadway; closes after 25 performances.

1961   Wins an Academy Award for best original screenplay for *Splendor in the Grass*. Adapts James Leo Herlihy's novel *All Fall Down* to the screen.

1962   Moves to Los Angeles, California. Does some lecturing on the theater arts.

1963   *Natural Affection* produced on Broadway unsuccessfully.

1964   NBC-TV Bob Hope Chrysler Theater presents Inge's *Out on the Outskirts of Town* starring Anne Bancroft.

1965   Writes film, *Bus Riley's Back in Town*. Inge demands removal of his name from credits after dispute with Universal Pictures. Screen credit given to "Walter Gage."

1966   *Where's Daddy?* produced on Broadway unsuccessfully.

1970   Writes *The Last Pad*. Publishes *Good Luck, Miss Wyckoff*, his first novel.

1971   Publishes *My Son is a Splendid Driver*, his second novel.

1973   Admitted to UCLA Medical Center for treatment of an overdose of barbiturates, 2 June. Transferred to psychiatric unit, 3 June. Signs himself out of hospital, 5 June. Commits suicide at his home in Los Angeles, 10 June.

We know very little about a talent
till we know where it grew up.

—*Henry James*

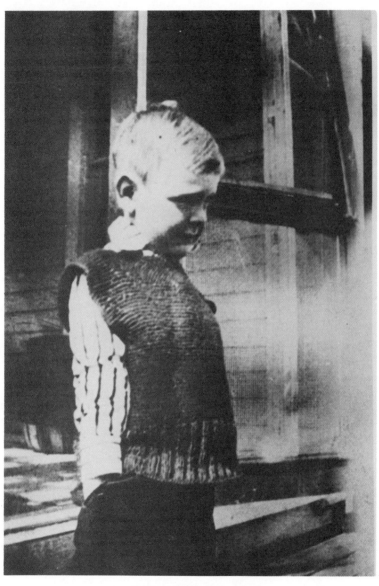
William Inge, circa 1920
(Courtesy of The William Inge Collection,
Independence Community College, Independence, Kansas)

Kim Novak with nine-year-old Patty Kay Welch,
on location at Halstead, Kansas, May-June 1955
(Courtesy of Mr. Kerry Welch)

Rosalind Russell during location shooting of *Picnic* at Halstead, Kansas, May-June 1955 (Courtesy of Mr. Harold S. Hall, Mrs. Frances Gehne, and Dr. Irene A. Koeneke)

Betty Field, seated left, and Susan Strasberg, standing right, during location shooting of *Picnic* at Halstead, Kansas, May-June 1955 (Courtesy of Mr. Harold S. Hall, Mrs. Frances Gehne, and Dr. Irene A. Koeneke)

The PLAYBILL
for The Booth Theatre

COME BACK, LITTLE SHEBA

PICNIC

The Music Box

Under Management of Irving Berlin and Lee Shubert

THE · PLAYBILL · A · WEEKLY · PUBLICATION · OF · PLAYBILL · INCORPORATED

Week beginning Monday, April 13, 1953 • Matinees Thursday and Saturday

IN THE EVENT OF AN AIR RAID ALARM REMAIN IN YOUR SEATS AND OBEY THE INSTRUCTIONS OF THE MANAGEMENT.—HERBERT R. O'BRIEN, DIRECTOR OF CIVIL DEFENSE.

THE THEATRE GUILD and JOSHUA LOGAN

Present

PICNIC

a new play by

WILLIAM INGE

with

RALPH MEEKER   JANICE RULE
EILEEN HECKART   KIM STANLEY   ARTHUR O'CONNELL
RUTH McDEVITT   PAUL NEWMAN

and

PEGGY CONKLIN

Directed by

JOSHUA LOGAN

Setting and Lighting by JO MIELZINER

Costumes by Mildred Trebor

CAST

(in order of appearance)

HELEN POTTS	RUTH McDEVITT
HAL CARTER	RALPH MEEKER
MILLIE OWENS	KIM STANLEY

I
Works by William Inge

THESIS

1. "David Belasco and the Age of Photographic Realism in the American Theatre." Master's thesis in English, George Peabody College for Teachers, Nashville, Tennessee, 1938.

PREFACES, INTRODUCTIONS, AND FOREWORDS

2. "Foreword." In *Four Plays by William Inge*. New York: Random House, 1958 (item 87), pp. v-x.

3. "Introduction." In *The Plains States*. New York: Time-Life Books, 1968.

4. "The Taste of Success: Excerpt from *Four Plays by William Inge*." In *American Playwrights on Drama*, pp. 127-133. Edited by Horst Frenz. New York: Hill and Wang, 1965.

PUBLISHED PLAYS

1950   *Come Back, Little Sheba*

5. *Come Back, Little Sheba*. New York: Random House, 1950. First publication.

6. *Come Back, Little Sheba*. New York: Samuel French, 1951. Acting edition.

7. *Come Back, Little Sheba*. London: Random House, 1952.

8. "*Come Back, Little Sheba*." In *Best American Plays, Third Series--1945-1951*, pp. 251-280. Edited by John Gassner. New York: Crown Publishers, 1952.

9. "*Come Back, Little Sheba.*" In *The Burns Mantle Best Plays of 1949-1950 and the Yearbook of the Drama in America,* pp. 173-196. Edited by John Chapman. New York: Dodd, Mead and Company, 1950.
    A condensation.

10. "*Come Back, Little Sheba.*" In *Contemporary Drama: Fifteen Plays, American, English, and Irish, European,* pp. 453-481. Edited by Ernest Bradley Watson and Benfield Pressy. New York: Charles Scribner's Sons, 1959.

11. "*Come Back, Little Sheba.*" In *Four Plays by William Inge.* New York: Random House, 1958 (item 87), pp. 1-69.

12. "*Come Back, Little Sheba.*" In *Modern Drama for Analysis,* pp. 95-166. Edited by Paul M. Cubeta. New York: Random House, 1967.

13. "*Come Back, Little Sheba.*" In *New Voices in the American Theatre,* pp. 227-299. Modern Library of the World's Best Books, No. 259. New York: The Modern Library, 195

14. "*Come Back, Little Sheba.*" In *Plays of Our Times,* pp. 409-468. Edited by Bennett Cerf. New York: Random House, 1967.

15. "*Come Back, Little Sheba.*" *Theatre Arts,* November 1950, pp. 60-88.

1950   *To Bobolink, for Her Spirit*

16. "*To Bobolink, for Her Spirit.*" In *Eleven Short Plays.* New York: Dramatists Play Service, 1962 (item 86), pp. 14-27.
     First publication.

17. "*To Bobolink, for Her Spirit.*" In *Kansas Renaissance,* pp. 49-57. Edited by Warren Kliewer and Stanley J. Solomon. Introduction by Allen Crafton. Lawrence, Kansas: Coronado Publications, 1961.

18. "*To Bobolink, for Her Spirit.*" In *The Mentor Book of Short Plays.* Edited by Richard H. Goldstone. New York New American Library, 1969.

19. *"To Bobolink, for Her Spirit."* In *ND12: New Directions in Prose and Poetry*, pp. 528-534. A New Directions Book. New York: James Laughlin, 1950.

20. *"To Bobolink, for Her Spirit."* In *Summer Brave and Eleven Short Plays*. New York: Random House, 1962 (item 89), pp. 115-127.

21. *"To Bobolink, for Her Spirit."* In *A Variety of Short Plays*. Edited by John C. Schweitzer. New York: Scribner's, 1966.

1953   *Picnic*

22. *Picnic*. New York: Random House, 1953.
    First publication.

23. *Picnic*. New York: Dramatists Play Service, 1955.
    Acting edition.

24. *Picnic*. New York: Bantam Books, 1956.

25. *"Picnic."* In *Best American Plays, Fourth Series--1951-1957*, pp. 211-244. Edited by John Gassner. New York: Crown Publishers, 1958.

26. *"Picnic."* In *The Best Plays of 1952-1953*, pp. 191-211. Edited by Louis Kronenberger. New York: Dodd, Mead and Company, 1953.
    A condensation.

27. *"Picnic."* In *Critics' Choice: New York Drama Critics' Circle Prize Plays, 1935-1955*, pp. 570-603. Edited by Jack Gaver. New York: Hawthorn Books, 1955.

28. *"Picnic."* In *Four Plays by William Inge*. New York: Random House, 1958 (item 87), pp. 71-148.

29. *"Picnic."* In *Great Scenes from the World Theatre*. Volume II. Edited by James L. Steffensen, Jr. New York: Discus Books, 1968.
    Selected scenes.

30. *"Picnic." Theatre Arts*, April 1954, pp. 34-61.

31. *"Picnic."* In *Theatre, 1953.* Edited by John Chapman.
      A condensation.

Translations

32. *Picnic.* Greek Translation by Marios Pioritis. Athens:
      Atlantic, 1958.

33. *"Picnic."* Italian Translation by Mino Roli. *Il Drama*
      231 (December 1955): 17–44.

34. *Picnic.* Japanese Translation by Hiroshi Trajima. Tokyo:
      Kwade Shobo, 1955.

35. *"Picnic."* In *Teatro Norteamericano Contemporaneo,*
      pp. 413–490. Spanish Translation by Juan Garcia-Puente.
      Madrid: Aguilar, 1961.

1955   *Bus Stop*

36. *Bus Stop.* New York: Random House, 1955.
      First publication.

37. *Bus Stop.* New York: Dramatists Play Service, 1955.
      Acting edition.

38. *Bus Stop.* New York: Bantam Books, 1956.

39. *"Bus Stop."* In *Best American Plays, Fourth Series--*
      1951-1957, pp. 245–277. Edited by John Gassner. New
      York: Crown Publishers, 1958.

40. *"Bus Stop."* In *Best Plays of 1954-1955,* pp. 267–287.
      Edited by Louis Kronenberger. New York: Dodd, Mead and
      Company, 1955.
      A condensation.

41. *"Bus Stop."* In *Four Plays by William Inge.* New York:
      Random House, 1958 (item 87), pp. 149–219.

42. *"Bus Stop."* *Theatre Arts,* October 1956, pp. 33–56.

43. *"Bus Stop."* In *Theatre, 1955,* pp. 115–135. Edited by
      John Chapman. New York: Random House, 1955.
      A condensation.

Published Plays

Translation

44. "*Bus Stop.*" In *Toneedfonds Maestro.* Volume 349. Dutch
    Translation by Alfred Pleiter. Amsterdam: Strengholt,
    1956.

1958   *The Dark at the Top of the Stairs*

45. *The Dark at the Top of the Stairs.* New York: Random
    House, 1958.
       First publication.

46. *The Dark at the Top of the Stairs.* New York: Bantam
    Books, 1958.

47. *The Dark at the Top of the Stairs.* New York: Dramatists
    Play Service, 1960.
       Acting edition.

48. *The Dark at the Top of the Stairs.* London: W. Heinemann,
    1960.

49. "*The Dark at the Top of the Stairs.*" In *Best American
    Plays, Fifth Series--1957-1963*, pp. 105-142. Edited
    by John Gassner. New York: Crown Publishers, 1963.

50. "*The Dark at the Top of the Stairs.*" In *The Best Plays
    of 1957-1958*, pp. 161-181. Edited by Louis Kronenberger.
    New York: Dodd, Mead and Company, 1958.
       A condensation.

51. "*The Dark at the Top of the Stairs.*" In *Broadway's Best,
    1958*, pp. 106-114. Edited by John Chapman. New York:
    Doubleday, 1958.
       A condensation.

52. "*The Dark at the Top of the Stairs.*" In *Four Plays by
    William Inge.* New York: Random House, 1958 (item 87),
    pp. 221-304.

53. "*The Dark at the Top of the Stairs.*" In *Great Scenes from
    the World Theatre.* Volume II. Edited by James L.
    Steffensen, Jr. New York: Discus Books, 1968.
       Selected scenes.

54. "*The Dark at the Top of the Stairs.*" In *Six American
    Plays for Today.* Edited by Bennett Cerf. Modern Li-
    brary of the World's Best Books, No. 38. New York:
    The Modern Library, 1961.

55. "*The Dark at the Top of the Stairs.*" *Theatre Arts*,
     September 1959, pp. 33-60.

1958   *Glory in the Flower*

56. "*Glory in the Flower.*" In *Twenty-four Favorite One-Act
     Plays*, pp. 133-150. Edited by Bennett Cerf and Van H.
     Cartmell. New York: Doubleday, 1958.

1959   *The Mall*

57. "*The Mall.*" In *Eleven Short Plays*. New York: Dramatists
     Play Service, 1962 (item 86), pp. 108-122.
     Acting edition.

58. "*The Mall.*" *Esquire*, January 1959, pp. 75-78.
     First publication.

59. "*The Mall.*" In *Summer Brave and Eleven Short Plays*. New
     York: Random House, 1962 (item 89), pp. 255-275.

1959   *The Tiny Closet*

60. "*The Tiny Closet.*" In *The Best Short Plays, 1958-1959*,
     pp. 33-43. Edited by Margaret Mayorga. Boston:
     Beacon Press, 1959.
     First publication.

61. "*The Tiny Closet.*" In *Eleven Short Plays*. New York:
     Dramatists Play Service, 1962 (item 86), pp. 56-66.

62. "*The Tiny Closet.*" In *Summer Brave and Eleven Short Plays*
     New York: Random House, 1962 (item 89), pp. 187-200.

1960   *A Loss of Roses*

63. *A Loss of Roses*. New York: Random House, 1960.

64. *A Loss of Roses*. New York: Dramatists Play Service, 1963.
     Acting edition.

65. *A Loss of Roses*. New York: Bantam Books, 1963.

66. "*A Loss of Roses*." In *Broadway's Best, 1960: The Complete Record of the Theatrical Year*. Edited by John Chapman. New York: Doubleday, 1960.
    A condensation.

67. "*A Loss of Roses*." *Esquire*, January 1960, pp. 138-144.
    First publication.

68. "*A Loss of Roses*." In *Great Scenes from the World Theatre*. Volume II. Edited by James L. Steffensen, Jr. New York: Discus Books, 1958.
    Selected scenes.

1962   *The Sounds of Triumph*

69. "*The Sounds of Triumph*" [Revised as "*The Strains of Triumph*"]. In *Eleven Short Plays*. New York: Dramatists Play Service, 1962 (item 86), pp. 130-142.
    Acting edition.

70. "*The Sounds of Triumph*." In *Plays as Experience: One-Act Plays for the Secondary School*, pp. 174-189. Edited by Irwin J. Zachar. Revised edition. New York: Odyssey Press, 1962.

71. "*The Sounds of Triumph*" [Revised as "*The Strains of Triumph*"]. In *Summer Brave and Eleven Short Plays*. New York: Random House, 1962 (item 89), pp. 282-299.

1962   *Summer Brave*

71a. "*Summer Brave*." In *Summer Brave and Eleven Short Plays*. New York: Random House, 1962 (item 89), pp. 1-113.

1962   *People in the Wind*

72. "*People in the Wind*." In *Summer Brave and Eleven Short Plays*. New York: Random House, 1962 (item 86), pp. 129-147.

1962   *Bus Riley's Back in Town*

73. "*Bus Riley's Back in Town*." In *Summer Brave and Eleven Short Plays*. New York: Random House, 1962 (item 86), pp. 213-239.

1962   *A Social Event*

74. "*A Social Event*." In *Summer Brave and Eleven Short Plays*.
     New York: Random House, 1962 (item 86), pp. 149-159.

1962   *The Boy in the Basement*

75. "*The Boy in the Basement*." In *Summer Brave and Eleven
     Short Plays*. New York: Random House, 1962 (item 86),
     pp. 161-185.

1962   *Memory of Summer*

76. "*Memory of Summer*." In *Summer Brave and Eleven Short
     Plays*. New York: Random House, 1962 (item 86), pp.
     201-212.

1962   *The Rainy Afternoon*

77. "*The Rainy Afternoon*." In *Summer Brave and Eleven Short
     Plays*. New York: Random House, 1962 (item 86), pp. 241-
     254.

1962   *An Incident at the Standish Arms*

78. "*An Incident at the Standish Arms*." In *Summer Brave and
     Eleven Short Plays*. New York: Random House, 1962 (item
     86), pp. 275-282.

1963   *Natural Affection*

79. *Natural Affection*. New York: Random House, 1963.
        First publication.

1966   *Where's Daddy?*

80. *Where's Daddy?* New York: Random House, 1966.
        First publication.

81. *Where's Daddy?* New York: Dramatists Play Service, 1966.
        Acting edition.

1968   *The Call*

82. "*The Call*." In *Two Short Plays: The Call, and A Murder*,
        pp. 3-19. New York: Dramatists Play Service, 1968.
        Contains item 83. First publication.

1968   *A Murder*

83. "*A Murder*." In *Two Short Plays: The Call, and A Murder*,
        pp. 21-46. New York: Dramatists Play Service, 1968.
        Contains item 82. First publication.

1968   *The Disposal*

84. "*The Disposal*." In *The Best Short Plays of the World
        Theatre, 1958-1967*. Edited by Stanley Richards. New
        York: Crown Publishers, 1968.
        First publication.

1969   *Midwestern Manic*

85. "*Midwestern Manic*." In *Best Short Plays, 1969*. Edited
        by Stanley Richards. Philadelphia: Chilton, 1969.
        First publication.

                      Collected Plays

86. *Eleven Short Plays*. New York: Dramatists Play Service,
        1962.
            Contains items 16, 57, 61, 69.
            Contents: "*To Bobolink, for Her Spirit*," pp. 3-13;
        "*People in the Wind*," pp. 14-27; "*A Social Event*,"
        pp. 28-36; "*The Boy in the Basement*," pp. 37-55; "*The
        Tiny Closet*," pp. 56-66; "*Memory of Summer*," pp. 67-76;
        "*Bus Riley's Back in Town*," pp. 77-96; "*The Rainy
        Afternoon*," pp. 96-107; "*The Mall*," pp. 108-122; "*An
        Incident at the Standish Arms*," pp. 123-129; "*The
        Strains of Triumph*," pp. 130-142.
            Acting edition of *Summer Brave and Eleven Short Plays*.

87.   *Four Plays by William Inge*. New York: Random House,
          1958.
              Contains items 2, 11, 28, 41, 52.
              Contents: Foreword by William Inge, pp. v-x; *Come
          Back, Little Sheba*, pp. 1-69; *Picnic*, pp. 71-148;
          Bus Stop, pp. 149-219; *The Dark at the Top of the
          Stairs*, pp. 221-304; "About the Author," p. 305.
              First publication.

88.   *Four Plays by William Inge*. London: William Heinemann,
          1960.

89.   *Summer Brave and Eleven Short Plays*. New York: Random
          House, 1962.
              Contains items 20, 59, 62, 71, 71a, 72-78.
              Contents: "*Summer Brave*," pp. 1-113; "*To Bobolink,
          for Her Spirit*," pp. 115-127; "*People in the Wind*,"
          pp. 129-147; "*A Social Event*," pp. 149-159; "*The Boy
          in the Basement*," pp. 161-185; "*The Tiny Closet*,"
          pp. 187-200; "*Memory of Summer*," pp. 201-212; "*Bus
          Riley's Back in Town*," pp. 213-239; "*The Rainy After-
          noon*," pp. 241-254; "*The Mall*," pp. 255-275; "*An
          Incident at the Standish Arms*," pp. 275-282; "*The
          Strains of Triumph*," pp. 282-299.
              First publication.

Translation

90.   *Summer Brave and Eleven Short Plays*. Greek Translation
          by E. Lonei-Christides. Athens: Atlantis, 1958.

                        PUBLISHED SCREENPLAY WRITTEN BY
                               WILLIAM INGE

91.   *Splendor in the Grass: A Screenplay*. New York: Bantam
          Books, 1961.

92.   *Splendor in the Grass: Stage Adaptation*. Adapted by
          F. Andrew Leslie. New York: Dramatists Play Service,
          1966.
              Acting edition.

NOVELS BY WILLIAM INGE

93. *Good Luck, Miss Wyckoff*. Boston and Toronto: Little, Brown and Company, 1970.

94. *Good Luck, Miss Wyckoff*. London: Deutsch, 1971.

95. *Good Luck, Miss Wyckoff*. New York: Bantam Books, 1971.

96. *My Son is a Splendid Driver*. Boston and Toronto: Little, Brown and Company, 1971.

ARTICLES WRITTEN BY WILLIAM INGE

97. "The American Scene." *Glamour*, May 1962, p. 111.

98. "Concerning Labels: 'Most Promising Playwright' Discusses Handicaps Imposed by Designation." *New York Times*, 23 July 1950, sec. 2, p. 1.

99. "Forgotten Anger." *Theatre Arts*, August 1958, p. 19.

100. "How Do You Like Your Chopin?" *New York Times*, 27 February 1955, sec. 2, pp. 1, 3.

101. "Instant Sympathy." *Show*, March 1962, pp. 92-93.

102. "More on the Playwright's Mission." *Theatre Arts*, August 1958, p. 19.

103. "On New York--And a New Play." *New York Herald Tribune*, 27 February 1966, pp. 27, 37.

104. "One Man's Experience in Living." *New York Times*, 27 July 1958, sec. 2, p. 1. An excerpt from the Foreword to *Four Plays by William Inge*.

105. "*Picnic*: From 'Front Porch' to Broadway." *Theatre Arts*, April 1954, pp. 32-33. Annotated on p. 56.

106. "*Picnic*: Of Women; Variety of Feminine Types in a Small Town Will be Seen in a New Play." *New York Times*, 15 February 1953, sec. 2, p. 3.

107. "Schizophrenic Wonder: An Analysis of *Come Back, Little Sheba*." *Theatre Arts*, May 1950, pp. 22-23.

108. "Writing for Films." *Playbill for the 46th Street Theatre*, 16 October 1961, pp. 5-15.

REVIEWS WRITTEN FOR THE
ST. LOUIS STAR-TIMES, 1943-1946

109. "Light-hearted 'Sunny' draws 9,000 to Municipal Opera," 15 June 1943, p. 8.

110. "Largest opening night crowd cheers popular 'Rose Marie,'" 22 June 1943, p. 12.

111. "'Quick turn' comic. Leonard Elliott is a mimic of things and ideas--such as boogie woogie, and opera," 26 June 1943, p. 9.

112. "Boogie-woogie moves uptown. Two piano aces 'give out' at Club here," 26 June 1943, p. 10.

113. "'Sons o' Guns' opening draws 9,500 to Municipal Opera," 29 June 1943, p. 12.

114. "Woman catcher. He floats through the air with the greatest of ease," 3 July 1943, p. 9. Review of *The Chocolate Soldier*.

115. "Year's biggest opening-night crowd sees 'Chocolate Soldier,'" 6 July 1943, p. 9.

116. "Roof top theater deals in arsenic again tonight," 6 July 1943, p. 19. Review of *Arsenic and Old Lace*.

117. "Harmless people--these mystery writers except when they keep you in suspense," 10 July 1943, p. 9. Interview with Isabel Taylor.

118. "Steindel praised for work at Little Symphony concert," 10 July 1943, p. 10.

119. "10,000 relish elaborate staging of 'The Great Waltz,'" 13 July 1943, p. 6.

120. "The real Macauley Muny opera star decides he's too
      versatile for own good," 13 July 1943, p. 16.

121. "Barracks soldiers encored at Little Symphony concert,"
      17 July 1943, p. 10.

122. "Gallery of Van Gogh paintings in Dutch art exhibit here,"
      17 July 1943, p. 10.

123. "The Record Album. D'Indy's Symphony among new wax re-
      leases of month," 17 July 1943, p. 10.

124. "On the Screen," 23 July 1943, p. 15.

125. "2,000 at Little Symphony concert encore Jean Browning,"
      24 July 1943, p. 10.

126. "Policeman has night in Muny opera," 26 July 1943, p. 17.

127. "Little Symphony winds up with brilliant concert," 31
      July 1943, p. 10.

128. "'Babes in Toyland' fantasy delights audience of 10,500,"
      3 August 1943, p. 10.

129. "On the Screen," 6 August 1943, p. 17.

130. "Met Star Irra Petina scores hit as Muny's 'Merry Widow,'"
      10 August 1943, p. 10.

131. "He [Chu Chin Chow] turned misfortune into fortune," 12
      August 1943, p. 19.

132. "On the Screen," 13 August 1943, p. 18.

133. "'Dark Eyes' one of best performances," 16 August 1943,
      p. 10.

134. "Muny opera closing season spectacularly. 'Chu Chin
      Chow' magnificent, entertaining," 17 August 1943, p. 17.

135. "On the Screen," 22 August 1943, p. 19.

136. "On the Screen," 27 August 1943, p. 6.

137. "At the opera. Future bright for Park stars as Jubilee
      season draws to close," 28 August 1943, p. 10.

138. "The Record Album. Beethoven and Telemann works on new
       disc sets," 28 August 1943, p. 10.

139. "Virile collection of army art displayed at City Art
       Museum," 31 August 1943, p. 14.

140. "On the Screen," 3 September 1943, p. 20.

141. "Spanish-Irish Margo dons oriental make-up in film
       [Behind the Rising Sun]," 9 September 1943, p. 17.

142. "On the Screen," 10 September 1943, p. 20.

143. "On the Screen," 17 September 1943, p. 22.

144. "On the Screen," 24 September 1943, p. 21.

145. "On the Screen," 1 October 1943, p. 23.

146. "The Record Album. Beethoven's 'Archduke' on new wax
       set," 3 October 1943, p. 11.

147. "Illinois artist's work placed on exhibit here," 5
       October 1943, p. 15.

148. "On the Screen," 8 October 1943, p. 21.

149. "On the Screen," 15 October 1943, p. 21.

150. "On the Screen," 22 October 1943, p. 20.

151. "'Tomorrow the World' has message on post-war Nazis,"
       24 October 1943, editorial section, p. 9.

152. "Missouri artists in fine show," 29 October 1943, p. 18.

153. "On the Screen," 29 October 1943, p. 19.

154. "On the Screen," 5 November 1943, p. 20.

155. "Near capacity crowd sees return of the 'Corn is Green,'"
       8 November 1943, p. 14.

156. "Opening symphony program honors memory of Becker," 8
       November 1943, p. 14.

157. "'For Whom the Bells Toll' [sic] shows movies can be art,"
       9 November 1943, p. 14.

158. "3,700 hear Philharmonic's first concert," 12 November
     1943, p. 11.

159. "On the Screen," 12 November 1943, p. 20.

160. "'Life with Father' still proves enjoyable in American
     return," 15 November 1943, p. 4.

161. "Pinza sings brilliantly but selections are disappoint-
     ing," 17 November 1943, p. 12.

162. "On the Screen," 19 November 1943, p. 18.

163. "'Mikroskosmos Suite' intriguing and evocative in
     premier," 22 November 1943, p. 8.

164. "'The Army Play by Play' is variety show, G.I. style,"
     23 November 1943, p. 7.

165. "Soldiers by day ... Actors by night. Strictly G.I. cast
     gives 'Command' performance every evening," 24 November
     1943, p. 14.

166. "On the Screen," 26 November 1943, p. 18.

167. "'Porgy and Bess' enjoyable as ever at the American,"
     27 November 1943, editorial section, p. 9.

168. "String quartet launching new season," 27 November 1943,
     p. 11.

169. "Little Theatre presents satire on success-conscious
     20's," 3 December 1943, p. 18.

170. "On the Screen," 3 December 1943, p. 20.

171. "Kipnis ill, program is reconstructed," 6 December 1943,
     p. 21.

172. "On the Screen," 10 December 1943, p. 21.

173. "'Billy the Kid' a big hit at Ballet Theater," 11
     December 1943, p. 11.

174. "Ballet Theater ends visit with new numbers," 13 December
     1943, p. 21.

175. "'Sons o' Fun' is party with Olsen and Johnson as hosts,"
      14 December 1943, p. 21.

176. "Comedian Besser clicks but 'not so fa-a-a-st, you,'"
      16 December 1943, p. 17.

177. "On the Screen," 17 December 1943, p. 17.

178. "Hortense Monath has upset musical tradition," 18 December
      1943, magazine section, p. 11.

179. "Miss Monath gives sensitive performance," 20 December
      1943, p. 19.

180. "Young artist burns midnight oil," 22 December 1943,
      p. 13.

181. "On the Screen," 24 December 1943, p. 10.

182. "U. City boy in commendable performance," 27 December
      1943, p. 6.

183. "Karloff coming back Sunday with 'Arsenic and Old Lace,'"
      31 December 1943, p. 9.

184. "On the Screen," 31 December 1943, p. 9.

185. "'Arsenic and Old Lace' still killing," 3 January 1944,
      p. 6.

186. "Missourian's symphony shows rich melody," 10 January
      1944, p. 6.

187. "Ballet Russe has mastery of technique," 11 January 1944,
      p. 6.

188. "Ballet's 'Rodeo' rides high with audience," 12 January
      1944, p. 11.

189. "Little Theater Play depicts peace bid by Wilson," 15
      January 1944, p. 11.

190. "Symphony plays music of Rachmaninoff," 17 January 1944,
      p. 6.

191. "'Blithe Spirit' has charm of this world," 18 January
      1944, p. 10.

192. "Joe Echasuiz brilliant in substitute role," 19 January
      1944, p. 4.

193. "'Tobacco Road,' on final tour, emphasizes comedy," 24
      January 1944, p. 4.

194. "Personalities in St. Louis. Walton and O'Roarke ...
      puppeteers. Margett Marbod ... actress," 26 January
      1944, p. 16.

195. "On the Screen," 4 February 1944, p. 14.

196. "The Record Album. Music of Gabriel Faure, noted teacher-
      composer, re-issued," 5 February 1944, p. 11.

197. "'Stolz' concert of Viennese music glitters," 5 February
      1944, p. 11.

198. "Record crowd hears excellent program by Marian Anderson,"
      9 February 1944, p. 6.

199. "On the Screen," 11 February 1944, p. 21.

200. "Wyndham Lewis ... English artist and author. Criticism
      established his reputation," 16 February 1944, p. 14.

201. "On the Screen," 18 February 1944, p. 19.

202. "The Record Album. Chausson and Debussy featured in new
      sets," 19 February 1944, p. 8.

203. "On the Screen," 25 February 1944, p. 17.

204. "'Three is a Family' brings babies, laughs to American,"
      28 February 1944, p. 6.

205. "On the Screen," 3 March 1944, p. 19.

206. "Symphony lets hair down. Beer and hot dogs vie with
      music at pension concert," 4 March 1944, p. 9.

207. "Girl violinist makes a hit at symphony," 6 March 1944,
      p. 4.

208. "On the Screen," 10 March 1944, p. 18.

209. "The Record Album. Beethoven's quartet No. 15 in new
      platter version," 11 March 1944, p. 9.

210. "'Tobacco Road' back with 3 new faces," 14 March 1944,
      p. 8.

211. "On the Screen," 17 March 1944, p. 21.

212. "William Kappel exciting in piano recital," 18 March
      1944, p. 9.

213. "'Good Night Ladies' put beauties first," 20 March
      1944, p. 6.

214. "Gould leads orchestra in light program," 20 March
      1944, p. 6.

215. "Ice-capades is fast moving, elaborate and amazing
      show," 22 March 1944, p. 11.

216. "Horowitz shows vast talent range," 24 March 1944, p. 10.

217. "On the Screen," 24 March 1944, p. 21.

218. "'Scandals' show at Fox has entertaining acts, fancy
      girls," 25 March 1944, p. 9.

219. "Chinese 'Little Jacket' is best Little Theater Play of
      year," 31 March 1944, p. 11.

220. "On the Screen," 31 March 1944, p. 21.

221. "'Kiss and Tell' light-hearted and amusing," 4 April
      1944, p. 6.

222. "On the Screen," 7 April 1944, p. 17.

223. "Hildegarde puts on her act at Chase," 11 April 1944,
      p. 6.

224. "On the Screen," 14 April 1944, p. 17.

225. "Coe Glade glistens as Carmen in lusty, spirited opera
      here," 15 April 1944, p. 9.

226. "On the Screen," 21 April 1944, p. 18.

227. "Last play of season at American," 25 April 1944, p. 8.

228. "'Dr. Wassell' premiere held at Little Rock," 27 April
      1944, p. 20.

229. "Stolz conducts pop concert at auditorium," 3 May 1944, p. 10.

230. "'Papa is All' is amusing throughout," 4 May 1944, p. 19.

231. "On the Screen," 5 May 1944, p. 19.

232. "On the Screen," 12 May 1944, p. 18.

233. "Philharmonic ends season on high note," 12 May 1944, p. 20.

234. "Group 15 show at City Art Museum. Versatility is keynote of current exhibit," 25 May 1944, p. 9.

235. "On the Screen," 26 May 1944, p. 20.

236. "Army takes away stage career--but gives it back. Singing star on G.I. Pay," 27 May 1944, p. 9.

237. "At Municipal Opera. Operetta 'Open Road' to launch new season in Park Thursday," 27 May 1944, p. 9.

238. "On the Screen," 2 June 1944, p. 13.

239. "On the Screen," 9 June 1944, p. 21.

240. "Muny Opera has good understudy for any role. Introducing versatile mime ... Bernie West," 10 June 1944, p. 11.

241. "The Record Album. Gould's 'Latin American Symphonette' on wax," 10 June 1944, p. 11.

242. "Audience of 8,000 cheers light-hearted 'Good News,'" 13 June 1944, p. 10.

243. "'Eve of St. Mark' converted into effective screen drama," 14 June 1944, p. 8.

244. "'Hitler Gang' film at Missouri is expert documentation," 16 June 1944, p. 20.

245. "Little Symphony returns for the summer. 'Music Under the Stars,'" 17 June 1944, p. 9.

246. "Record 1944 crowd of 10,000 see pleasing 'Vagabond King,'" 20 June 1944, p. 14.

247. "'Follow the Boys' praises Hollywood," 21 June 1944, p. 6.

248. "'Between Two Worlds,' film on life after death, is
      superior," 22 June 1944, p. 18.

249. "On the Screen," 23 June 1944, p. 8.

250. "10th Little Symphony season opens with pleasing program,"
      24 June 1944, p. 8.

251. "Victor Herbert's operetta 'Eileen' has musical appeal,"
      27 June 1944, p. 12.

252. "'Mask of Dimitrios' rated with 'Attack' as excellent,"
      28 June 1944, p. 14.

253. "Chapple conducts spirited Little Symphony concert,"
      1 July 1944, p. 9.

254. "'Hit the Deck' makes a hit; songs captivate audiences,"
      5 July 1944, p. 16.

255. "Deanna Durbin good in grim dramatic role," 6 July 1944,
      p. 17.

256. "Touhy film exciting story of past era," 7 July 1944,
      p. 15.

257. "Skill of Robert LaMarchina as cellist amazes audience,"
      8 July 1944, p. 9.

258. "Audience of 10,000 enjoys colorful 'Naughty Marietta,'"
      11 July 1944, p. 14.

259. "1,600 hear Little Symphony in well performed concert,"
      15 July 1944, p. 9.

260. "'Music in the Air' has hit tunes and fine cast,"
      18 July 1944, p. 12.

261. "Crosby and Barry Fitzgerald superb in warm-hearted
      'Going My Way,'" 20 July 1944, p. 14.

262. "'Hairy Ape' is usual film drama," 21 July 1944, p. 9.

263. "Wilson Robinson encored 3 times; 'Playing Zestful,'"
      22 July 1944, p. 9.

264. "Love angle criticized in 'Dr. Wassell,'" 26 July 1944,
     p. 6.

265. "Skelton film is lavish, light musical," 28 July 1944,
     p. 16.

266. "Mme. Parpari shows artistry as Little Symphony's soloist,"
     29 July 1944, p. 9.

267. "Maureen Cannon ideal as 'Irene' in appealing opera,"
     1 August 1944, p. 12.

268. "Trying days for Navy in Fox picture," 4 August 1944, p. 8.

269. "Dick Powell excellent in eerie comedy," 4 August 1944,
     p. 17.

270. "Dora Minkin, Bessie A. Noack encored in 2-piano concerto,"
     5 August 1944, p. 6.

271. "All-star cast and hit songs make 'Bohemian Girl' a
     success," 8 August 1944, p. 14.

272. "'Atlantic City,' new musical film at Fox," 9 August
     1944, p. 9.

273. "'Dragon Seed' an emotional story of Chinese at war,"
     11 August 1944, p. 19.

274. "Finale of Little Symphony finest concert of season,"
     12 August 1944, p. 9.

275. "Crowd of 10,200 applauds 'Red Mill,' children's treat,"
     15 August 1944, p. 8.

276. "9,000 brave rain to see lively, colorful 'Rio Rita,'"
     22 August 1944, p. 12.

277. "Municipal opera personalities: Watson Barratt ...
     scene designer," 23 August 1944, p. 14.

278. "'Sensations of 1945'--jitterbug and jive," 24 August
     1944, p. 12.

279. "'Janie' at Fox is refreshing, wholesome," 27 August
     1944, p. 6.

280. "'7th Cross' is sordid, but very good," 1 September 1944,
      p. 16.

281. "Film at Fox is another Sturges hit," 6 September 1944,
      p. 10.

282. "On the Screen," 8 September 1944, p. 21.

283. "'Step Lively,' with Sinatra, is diverting," 14 September
      1944, p. 10.

284. "Vivien Leigh appealing in Loew's film," 15 September 1944,
      p. 19.

285. "Sid Tomack a 'fixed' planet in Chase firmament. Comic
      star soars in the zodiac," 16 September 1944, p. 11.

286. "On the Screen," 22 September 1944, p. 9.

287. "ZaSu Pitts play spells good time," 2 October 1944, p. 16.

288. "'Waltz King' in jazzy version at American," 9 October
      1944, p. 16.

289. "'Arsenic and Old Lace' film takes slapstick turn,"
      9 October 1944, p. 19.

290. "Fox picture designed for bobby soxers," 11 October 1944,
      p. 20.

291. "Portia White gets ovation in recital here," 11 October
      1944, p. 20.

292. "'Bandwagon' show full of sting for G.O.P.," 12 October
      1944, p. 19.

293. "Ghost film at Loew's is entertaining," 13 October 1944,
      p. 20.

294. "This is Chicago. Visitory gets line on shows after a
      few headaches," 14 October 1944, p. 11.

295. "Tropical Revue is beautiful and exciting," 17 October
      1944, p. 10.

296. "Actress objects to 'best seller' stage plays," 18 October
      1944, p. 16.

297. "Community Theater's version of Greed legend entertaining,"
       19 October 1944, p. 10.

298. "Runyon humor missing in his latest movie," 19 October
       1944, p. 10.

299. "Wallace Beery in familiar role at Loew's," 20 October
       1944, p. 25.

300. "'Cherry Orchard' an expert blend of humor and pathos,"
       24 October 1944, p. 8.

301. "'Bride by Mistake' movie has light, humorous tone,"
       26 October 1944, p. 10.

302. "Loew's picture adapted from Chekhov's tale," 27 October
       1944, p. 21.

303. "'Wallflower' makes a hit with audience," 30 October 1944,
       p. 10.

304. "'Conspirators' is exciting spy drama." 1 November 1944,
       p. 9.

305. "'Master Race' again depicts Nazi bestiality," 2 November
       1944, p. 10.

306. "On the Screen," 3 November 1944, p. 21.

307. "Symphony excellent in first concerts," 6 November 1944,
       p. 10.

308. "Western film at Fox is wholesome," 8 November 1944, p. 24.

309. "Ethel Barrymore outstanding in tragic, yet beautiful
       film," 9 November 1944, p. 14.

310. "Gypsy film like opera without music," 10 November 1944,
       p. 21.

311. "St. Louis personalities. 'Tennessee' Williams, play-
       wright, author," 11 November 1944, p. 11.

312. "Ruth Gordon is brilliant comedienne in 'Over 21,'"
       14 November 1944, p. 16.

313. "'Brazil' film has aspect of travelogue," 15 November
       1944, p. 8.

314. "'Frenchman's Creek' runs into action," 16 November 1944,
      p. 20.

315. "'American Romance' is typical epic," 17 November 1944,
      p. 8.

316. "'Family Affair' scintillating in Symphony," 20 November
      1944, p. 8.

317. "Lily Pons and Kostelanetz to resume army camp tour,"
      21 November 1944, p. 5.

318. "'Life with Father' keeps its freshness," 21 November
      1944, p. 17.

319. "'Skating Vanities' returns in spectacular, lavish form,"
      22 November 1944, p. 5.

320. "New musical at Fox has usual mixture," 22 November 1944,
      p. 20.

321. "Kostelanetz, Lily Pons give fine concert," 24 November
      1944, p. 24.

322. "'Meet Me in St. Louis' is captivating," 24 November 1944,
      p. 24.

323. "Symphony shows shift in patrons' taste," 27 November
      1944, p. 6.

324. "Fox picture tries to 'plug' vaudeville," 29 November
      1944, p. 8.

325. "Miss Anderson outstanding in recital," 29 November 1944,
      p. 10.

326. "Audience likes new farce at American," 4 December 1944,
      p. 6.

327. "Three new art exhibits open here," 4 December 1944, p. 6.

328. "'Winged Victory' spectacular; placed on 'must see' list,"
      5 December 1944, p. 16.

329. "New film at Loew's stars Lana Turner," 8 December 1944,
      p. 20.

330. "Martyl's one-woman show features Mexico, originality,"
      11 December 1944, p. 6.

331. "The Record Album," 14 December 1944, p. 20.

332. "4,000 pupils attend their 2nd Symphony," 15 December
      1944, p. 8.

333. "2 Symphony concerts span 400 years," 18 December 1944,
      p. 8.

334. "Fox comedy entertaining and gay," 19 December 1944, p. 6.

335. "The Record Album," 21 December 1944, p. 14.

336. "'Rebecca' has fine acting and suspense," 26 December
      1944, p. 6.

337. "The Record Album," 28 December 1944, p. 12.

338. "Helen Hayes' acting superb in period drama, 'Harriet,'"
      2 January 1945, p. 6.

339. "Musical comedy ready to 'hit the road' to St. Louis.
      'Everything's up to date' in stage play 'Oklahoma,'"
      4 January 1945, p. 12.

340. "Ballet Theater blends classic and modern," 6 January
      1945, p. 11.

341. "Ballet Theater performances excellent," 8 January 1945,
      p. 6.

342. "Movie 'Winged Victory' better than on stage," 10 January
      1945, p. 8.

343. "Alan Ladd film popular, yet depressing," 11 January 1945,
      p. 7.

344. "The Record Album," 11 January 1945, p. 12.

345. "'Too big a gap between jazz and classics,' Leinsdorf
      says," 11 January 1945, p. 14.

346. "Guest conducts Symphony in Wagner music," 15 January
      1945, p. 6.

347. "Fritz Kreisler gives mellow performance," 17 January
      1945, p. 9.

348. "The Record Album," 18 January 1945, p. 16.

349. "'Skin of Our Teeth' one of best plays," 19 January
      1945, p. 6.

350. "Comedians help prince regain throne," 19 January 1945,
      p. 8.

351. "Barzin leads Symphony in Kessler work," 22 January
      1945, p. 6.

352. "'Here Comes the Waves' at Fox is lively satire,"
      24 January 1945, p. 6.

353. "Boyer, Dunne excellent in gay comedy," 25 January 1945,
      p. 9.

354. "The Record Album," 25 January 1945, p. 16.

355. "Chopin's life gets elaborate film handling," 26 January
      1945, p. 16.

356. "'Mikado' well sung at American," 29 January 1945, p. 6.

357. "The Record Album," 1 February 1945, p. 12.

358. "Ambassador thriller has good acting," 1 February 1945,
      p. 16.

359. "Argentinita's show colorful and exciting," 1 February
      1945, p. 16.

360. "Miss Grahame standout in 'Blonde Fever,'" 2 February
      1945, p. 6.

361. "Chapple leads Symphony in diverse works," 5 February
      1945, p. 4.

362. "Display of Feininger water colors opens," 5 February
      1945, p. 4.

363. "Ibsen's play at American still great," 5 February 1945,
      p. 4.

364. "'Pin-up Boy of Symphony' has a 'passion for jazz music,'"
      6 February 1945, p. 9.

365. "Lauren Bacall 'makes' new film at Fox," 7 February 1945,
      p. 7.

366. "Templeton gives brilliant and entertaining program,"
      7 February 1945, p. 7.

367. "'Keys of the Kingdom' impressive film story of priest
      in China," 8 February 1945, p. 18.

368. "Two good comedies at Loew's State," 9 February 1945, p. 10.

369. "Bernstein brilliant in two concerts," 12 February 1945,
      p. 4.

370. "'Kiss and Tell' durable as laugh-getter," 12 February
      1945, p. 4.

371. "'Sunday Dinner for a Soldier' warm, human and appealing,"
      15 February 1945, p. 17.

372. "Mitropoulos is dramatic as conductor," 15 February 1945,
      p. 18.

373. "Why be frightened? It's just a movie about a graveyard,"
      16 February 1945, p. 8.

374. "'Fighting Lady' film great war document," 17 February
      1945, p. 11.

375. "Bernstein applauded on modern works," 19 February 1945,
      p. 6.

376. "R.A.F. band gives spirited performance," 19 February
      1945, p. 6.

377. "Dick Powell is excellent in another good thriller,"
      21 February 1945, p. 9.

378. "The Record Album," 22 February 1945, p. 14.

379. "On the Screen," 23 February 1945, p. 19.

380. "3,000 hear Rubenstein and Symphony," 26 February 1945,
      p. 6.

381. "4,000 hear Iturbi play boogie woogie," 28 February 1945,
      p. 6.

382. "'Practically Yours' a light fast-moving comedy farce,"
      1 March 1945, p. 8.

383. "Golschmann, Manuhin in brilliant roles," 5 March 1945,
      p. 6.

384. "'Ramshackle Inn' returns; still funny," 5 March 1945,
      p. 6.

385. "'Dark Waters' a creepy murder mystery thriller,"
      8 March 1945, p. 12.

386. "Normal and abnormal mix at Loew's, Missouri films,"
      9 March 1945, p. 21.

387. "Romantic note ends season for Symphony," 12 March 1945,
      p. 6.

388. "'Searching Wind' a drama with fine cast and a wallop,"
      13 March 1945, p. 8.

389. "Horowitz gives season's best piano concert," 14 March
      1945, p. 8.

390. "'Roughly Speaking' humorous account of family's troubles,"
      15 March 1945, p. 8.

391. "'I'll be Seeing You,' a sad, but heartening wartime film,"
      16 March 1945, p. 12.

392. "10,000 see entertaining Ice-capades," 16 March 1945,
      p. 12.

393. "'Blossom Time' back, but a bit withered," 19 March 1945,
      p. 4.

394. "'Tree Grows in Brooklyn' is human, appealing film,"
      21 March 1945, p. 10.

395. "Resemblance to 'Gaslight' in Hedy's film," 22 March 1945,
      p. 8.

396. "'Blithe Spirit' returns, still a lot of fun," 27 March
      1945, p. 8.

397. "Lavish dances, little plot in London film," 29 March
      1945, p. 10.

398. "Tennessee Williams. Clayton man's play about family
      life here is a hit," 3 April 1945, p. 6.

399. "'Barbary Coast Place' shows fine acting," 5 April 1945,
      p. 10.

400. "Boy's dream mixed up in Missouri film," 6 April 1945,
      p. 10.

401. "Sonja Henie, Disney made good show," 12 April 1945, p. 10.

402. "'Aida,' jive both heard at auditorium," 13 April 1945,
      p. 12.

403. "New Loew's film stresses psychology," 13 April 1945,
      p. 12.

404. "2,800 see twin operas by San Carlo," 14 April 1945, p. 11.

405. "San Carlo Opera Company ends visit," 16 April 1945, p. 6.

406. "'Jacobowsky' is rated best of new plays," 17 April 1945,
      p. 10.

407. "'Hotel Berlin' has timely news interest," 18 April 1945,
      p. 10.

408. "6,000 find 'pop' concert diverting," 18 April 1945, p. 10.

409. "War problem in 'Enchanted Cottage' film," 19 April 1945,
      p. 10.

410. "Playhouse production entertaining," 20 April 1945, p. 18.

411. "Mae West show is fun sometimes," 24 April 1945, p. 8.

412. "'Yukon Belle' at Fox has good points," 25 April 1945,
      p. 8.

413. "Tallulah takes spotlight in 'Royal Scandal' on screen,"
      26 April 1945, p. 8.

414. "The Record Album," 26 April 1945, p. 16.

415. "Leo Law ... street painter. A masterpiece a minute is his speed," 27 April 1945, p. 18.

416. "'Dorian Gray,' famed shocker, is realistic and artistic," 27 April 1945, p. 20.

417. "Bach festival here makes a good start," 30 April 1945, p. 7.

418. "'One Touch of Venus' scintillating," 1 May 1945, p. 16.

419. "Shy Elizabeth Bergner steers clear of interviews and people. The Garbo of the stage," 1 May 1945, p. 16.

420. "Organist gives brilliant Bach festival recital," 3 May 1945, p. 8.

421. "The Record Album," 3 May 1945, p. 14.

422. "Bach choral, chamber music in festival," 4 May 1945, p. 10.

423. "New Missouri picture alive with corpses," 4 May 1945, p. 10.

424. "Elizabeth Bergner enchanting in 'The Two Mrs. Carrolls,'" 8 May 1945, p. 18.

425. "Jack Benny in different, screwball comedy at Fox," 9 May 1945, p. 8.

426. "On the Screen," 10 May 1945, p. 10.

427. "The Record Album," 10 May 1945, p. 18.

428. "Last Philharmonic concert played well and cheered," 11 May 1945, p. 21.

429. "Theater in wartime," 13 May 1945, p. 11.

430. "On the Screen," 16 May 1945, p. 9.

431. "On the Screen," 17 May 1945, p. 8.

432. "The Record Album," 17 May 1945, p. 14.

433. "On the Screen," 18 May 1945, p. 7.

434. "On the Screen," 24 May 1945, p. 8.

435. "The Record Album," 24 May 1945, p. 14.

436. "On the Screen," 31 May 1945, p. 16.

437. "The Record Album," 31 May 1945, p. 12.

438. "Film on Handel to start tonight at Art Theater," 2 June
       1945, p. 6.

439. "Good film version of Steinbeck story," 7 June 1945, p. 16.

440. "Cole Porter comedy in excellent hands. Muny Opera with
       'Jubilee,'" 8 June 1945, p. 19.

441. "Best seller on first try. Author who taught here sells
       'Rome Hanks' to movies," 11 June 1945, p. 5.

442. "Joan Fontaine shows skill in new role," 14 June 1945,
       p. 18.

443. "Cast makes 'O'Brien Girl' entertaining," 19 June 1945,
       p. 8.

444. "The Record Album," 21 June 1945, p. 14.

445. "'On Approval' highly intelligent comedy," 21 June 1945,
       p. 18.

446. "Herbert tunes sung expertly at Muny Opera," 26 June
       1945, p. 8.

447. "Artists run risks, too. Coast guardsman here says
       realism is the thing," 27 June 1945, p. 6.

448. "The Record Album," 28 June 1945, p. 14.

449. "'On Approval' proves box office success," 28 June 1945,
       p. 18.

450. "St. Louis Little Symphony in first concert," 30 June
       1945, p. 11.

451. "The Record Album," 5 July 1945, p. 4.

452. "Greer Garson in tailored role," 6 July 1945, p. 6.

453. "2,000 hear Joan Gale, Symphony," 7 July 1945, p. 11.

454. "'Cat, Fiddle' impressive for thirteen scenes," 10 July
      1945, p. 6.

455. "The Record Album," 12 July 1945, p. 12.

456. "Young pianist success with Symphony," 14 July 1945, p. 11.

457. "Cyril Smith is at the Fox 'singing' about old sow,"
      17 July 1945, p. 8.

458. "Season's best scene is in 'Pompadour,'" 17 July 1945,
      p. 8.

459. "Fred Allen in rib-tickling scenes," 19 July 1945, p. 18.

460. "Pep talk from Muny opera conductor. McArthur makes
      music," 20 July 1945, p. 17.

461. "'Melting Pot of Races.' Paul Muni, appearing here,
      lauds Negro music festival," 23 July 1945, p. 6.

462. "10,200 see 'Firefly' open week's run," 24 July 1945,
      p. 6.

463. "Muny's Romney Brent writes play, directs soldier shows,"
      25 July 1945, p. 8.

464. "The Record Album," 26 July 1945, p. 12.

465. "Jap suicide planes filmed in action," 26 July 1945, p. 16

466. "Steindel leads orchestra in varied works," 28 July 1945,
      p. 11.

467. "'Pink Lady' returns in gay fashion," 31 July 1945,
      p. 6.

468. "'Bell for Adano,' Gary Cooper provide good entertainment,
      2 August 1945, p. 6.

469. "The Record Album," 2 August 1945, p. 12.

470. "2,300 hear concert at Quadrangle," 4 August 1945, p. 11.

471. "Charm, color is keynote of 'Musketeers,'" 7 August 1945,
      p. 8.

472. "On the Screen," 9 August 1945, p. 14.

473. "The Record Album," 13 September 1945, p. 16.

474. "On the Screen," 13 September 1945, p. 21

475. "Artist had to 'take it' overseas. Howard Baer doesn't
      like sight of blood, but he's used to it," 14 September
      1945, p. 24.

476. "3,000 attend 'beer, pretzel' concert," 15 September
      1945, p. 11.

477. "Thriller opens 2-week run at American," 17 September
      1945, p. 8.

478. "On the Screen," 20 September 1945, p. 10.

479. "The Record Album," 20 September 1945, p. 18.

480. "On the Screen," 21 September 1945, p. 25.

481. "On the Screen," 27 September 1945, p. 12.

482. "The Record Album," 27 September 1945, p. 18.

483. "On the Screen," 4 October 1945, p. 15.

484. "On the Screen," 5 October 1945, p. 14.

485. "On the Screen," 11 October 1945, p. 15.

486. "The Record Album," 11 October 1945, p. 20.

487. "On the Screen," 12 October 1945, p. 12.

488. "On the Screen," 18 October 1945, p. 12.

489. "The Record Album," 18 October 1945, p. 22.

490. "On the Screen," 19 October 1945, p. 17.

491. "On the Screen," 25 October 1945, p. 11.

492. "The Record Album," 25 October 1945, p. 20.

493. "On the Screen," 1 November 1945, p. 12.

494. "On the Screen," 2 November 1945, p. 18.

495. "The Record Album," 8 November 1945, p. 24.

496. "On the Screen," 8 November 1945, p. 27.

497. "On the Screen," 9 November 1945, p. 23.

498. "The Record Album," 15 November 1945, p. 22.

499. "On the Screen," 16 November 1945, p. 20.

500. "The Record Album," 23 November 1945, p. 20.

501. "On the Screen," 29 November 1945, p. 14.

502. "The Record Album," 29 November 1945, p. 20.

503. "On the Screen," 30 November 1945, p. 21.

504. "The Record Album," 5 December 1945, p. 54.

505. "On the Screen," 7 December 1945, p. 22.

506. "On the Screen," 13 December 1945, p. 10.

507. "The Record Album," 13 December 1945, p. 22.

508. "The Record Album," 20 December 1945, p. 18.

509. "On the Screen," 26 December 1945, p. 10.

510. "The Record Album," 27 December 1945, p. 20.

511. "'Harvey' opens to full house at American," 2 January 1946, p. 10.

512. "On the Screen," 10 January 1946, p. 6.

513. "The Record Album," 10 January 1946, p. 18.

514. "On the Screen," 17 January 1946, p. 8.

515. "The Record Album," 17 January 1946, p. 18.

516. "Miss Woodward scores in role at Philharmonic," 18 January 1946, p. 16.

517. "On the Screen," 18 January 1946, p. 17.

518. "Miss Anderson excellent in recital here," 19 January 1946, p. 5.

519. "Rubinstein gives polished performance," 21 January 1946, p. 8.

520. "Fine concert by Chicago Symphony," 23 January 1946, p. 12.

521. "On the Screen," 23 January 1946, p. 14.

522. "On the Screen," 24 January 1946, p. 12.

523. "The Record Album," 24 January 1946, p. 18.

524. "On the Screen," 25 January 1946, p. 16.

525. "Szigeti gives stimulating performance," 26 January 1946, p. 5.

526. "Polish, finesse displayed here by Casadesus," 9 February 1946, p. 5.

II
Biographical Information

BOOKS, ARTICLES, SKETCHES,
AND BIOGRAPHICAL DICTIONARIES

527. Atkinson, Brooks. "A Haunted Playwright." *New York Times*, 11 June 1973, p. 38.

528. Aurthur, Robert Alan. "Hanging Out." *Esquire*, November 1973, pp. 42-52.

529. Beaufort, John. "Inge's Lyric Midwest." *Christian Science Monitor*, 16 June 1973, p. 5.

530. Biographical Sketch of William Inge. In *Current Biography: Who's News and Why*, June 1953, pp. 34-36.
      A basic biographical source.

531. Biography of William Inge. In *American Annual*, 1954, p. 343.

532. Biography of William Inge. *Time*, 16 December 1957, p. 42.

533. Bracker, Milton. "Boy Actor to Broadway Author." *New York Times*, 22 March 1953, pp. 1-3.
      An early biographical treatment of Inge.

534. "Brief Biographies of the Pulitzer Prize Winners in Letters and Journalism for 1953." *New York Times*, 5 May 1953, p. 24.

535. Brief Sketch of William Inge. In *Catalog Arts and Crafts of Kansas*, 1948, p. 117.

*   Brustein, Robert. "The Men-Taming Women of William Inge." *Harper's Magazine*, November 1958, pp. 52-57. Cited below as item 587.

536. Burgess, Charles E. "An American Experience: William Inge in St. Louis, 1943-1949." *Pennsylvania Language and Literature* 12 (Fall 1976): 438-469.

537. Candee, Marjorie Dent, ed. "Inge, William (Motter)."
      In *Current Biography: Who's News and Why, 1953.*
      New York: The H.W. Wilson Company, 1954, pp. 292-294.

538. "Candidates for Prizes; Nine Younger Playwrights."
      Vogue, May 1954, p. 135.

539. "A Conversation with Digby Diehl." *Transatlantic
      Review* 26 (Autumn 1967): 51-56. Also in *Behind the
      Scenes: Theater and Film Interviews from the Trans-
      atlantic Review*, pp. 108-115. Edited by Joseph J.
      McCrindle. New York: Holt, Rinehart and Winston, 1971.

540. "Defector." *Newsweek*, 14 May 1962, p. 110.
      Discusses Inge's move to California after his dis-
      illusionment with New York critics.

541. *Enciclopidia Dello Spettacolo*, 1959 ed., s.v. "William
      Inge."

542. Esterow, Milton. "News of the Rialto: Inge's Plans."
      New York Times, 17 June 1962, p. 1.

543. Etheridge, James M. "Inge, William Motter." In
      *Contemporary Authors: A Biographical Guide to Current
      Authors and Their Works*. Detroit: Gale Research
      Company, 1964, pp. 227-228.

*   Gould, Jean Rosalind. "William Inge." In *Modern
      American Playwrights*. New York: Dodd, Mead and
      Company, 1966 (item 608), pp. 264-272.

544. Groves, Gerald. "The Success of William Inge." *Critic*
      23 (December 1964-January 1965): 16-19.

545. Harrington, Grant W. Biographical Sketch of William
      Inge. In *Sigma Nu at Kansas University, 1884-1956*,
      1956, pp. 172-173.

546. Hoff, Dolores Dorn. "Toby: The Twilight of a Tradition."
      Theatre Arts, August 1958, p. 55.

547. Kunitz, Stanley J., and Colby, Vineta, eds. "Inge,
      William Motter." In *Twentieth Century Authors: First
      Supplement*. New York: H.W. Wilson Company, 1955,
      pp. 475-476.
      A basic biographical source.

548. Lewis, Allan. "The Emergent Deans--Kingsley, Inge, and Company." In *American Plays and Playwrights of the Contemporary Theatre*. New York: Crown Publishing, 1965, pp. 150-153, 195-196.

549. Lumley, Fredrick. "William Inge." In *New Trends in 20th Century Drama: A Survey Since Ibsen and Shaw*. New York: Oxford University Press, 1967, pp. 329-331.

550. *Magazine*, 27 September 1953, pp. 10-11.

551. Manley, Frances. "William Inge: A Bibliography." *American Book Collector* 16 (October 1965): 13-21.

552. Matlaw, Myron. "Inge, William (Motter)." In *Modern World Drama: An Encyclopedia*. New York: E.P. Dutton and Company, 1972, pp. 391-392.

553. McCarthy, Mary. "Americans, Realists, Playwrights." *Encounter* 17 (July 1961): 24-31.

554. *McGraw-Hill Encyclopedia of World Drama: An International Reference Work in Four Volumes*, 1972 ed., s.v. "Inge, William."

555. Melchinger, Siegried. "Inge, William." In *The Concise Encyclopedia of Modern Drama*, p. 218. Edited by Henry Popkin. New York: Horizon Press, 1964.

556. Millstein, Gilbert. "The Dark at the Top of William Inge." *Esquire*, August 1958, pp. 60-63.

557. Murphy, Josephine. "Broadway's White Hope." *Nashville Tennessean Magazine*, 20 September 1953, pp. 7-17. Very positive assessment of Inge and his work.

558. Nathan, George Jean. "William Inge." In *The Theatre in the Fifties*. New York: Alfred A. Knopf, 1953, pp. 71-76.

559. Nyren, Dorothy. "Inge, William." In *A Library of Literary Criticism*. New York: Ungar, 1960, pp. 244-246.

560. "*Picnic* Fills His Lunch Pail." *Alumni Magazine* (University of Kansas) 51 (March 1953): 6.

561. "[William Inge] Returns to K.U. as a Guest Lecturer."
      K.U. News Bureau Release, 26 January 1960.

562. Rigdon, Walter, ed. "Inge, William." In *The Biographical
      Encyclopedia and Who's Who of the American Theatre*.
      New York: James H. Heineman, Inc., 1966, p. 562.

563. Salem, James M. "Inge, William." In *Drury's Guide to
      Best Plays*, second edition. Metuchen, New Jersey:
      Scarecrow Press, 1969, pp. 197-200.

564. Schott, Webster. "Devious Path to a Career was Taken by
      a Mid-Western Teacher of Drama." *Kansas City Star*,
      16 September 1949, p. 22.

565. Shuman, R. Baird. *William Inge*. Twayne's United States
      Authors Series, No. 95. New York: Twayne Publishers,
      Inc., 1965.
           The only book-length study of Inge to date.

566. Smith, John J., ed. "Inge, William (Motter)." In *The
      Americana Annual: An Encyclopedia of the Events of 1953*.
      New York and Chicago: Americana Corporation, 1954, p. 343

567. "The Talk of the Town." *New Yorker*, 4 April 1953, pp. 24-
      25.
           Describes Inge's childhood and youthful years.

568. "Tender Insight: A Touch of Toby." *Life*, 6 January 1958,
      pp. 74-77.
           Discusses *The Dark at the Top of the Stairs* and the
      influence of his acting in Toby shows on his writing
      style.

569. "Theatre USA." *Theatre Arts*, October 1958, p. 54.

570. Vinson, James, ed. "Contemporary Dramatists." *St.
      Martins*, 1973, pp. 399-406.

571. Wager, Walter, ed. *The Playwrights Speak*. Introduction
      by Harold Clurman. New York: Dell Publishing Company,
      Delta Books, 1967, pp. xviii-xxi, 110-139.

572. Williams, Tennessee. "The Writing is Honest." In *The
      Dark at the Top of the Stairs*. By William Inge. New
      York: Random House, 1958 (item 45), pp. vii-ix. Also
      in *The Passionate Playgoer*, pp. 246-249. Edited by
      George Oppenheimer. New York: Viking Press, 1958.

OBITUARIES

573. *Current Biographies Yearbook*, 1973, p. 456.

574. *Current Biography*, July 1973, p. 43.

575. *Newsweek*, 25 June 1973, p. 45.

576. *Time*, 25 June 1973, p. 71.

577. "William Inge, Playwright is Dead." *New York Times*,
      11 June 1973, p. 1.

POST-MORTEMS

578. "Playwright W. Gibson Comments on His Friendship with
      Late Playwright William Inge." *New York Times*, 24
      July 1973, p. 35.

579. "Tennessee Williams' Tribute to Playwright William Inge,
      Who Died on June 10." *New York Times*, 1 July 1973,
      sec. 2, p. 3.

580. "William Inge is Found Dead on June 10, After Apparently
      Committing Suicide; Was 60." *New York Times*, 11 June
      1973, p. 2.

581. "William Inge Leaves Estate of Over $50,000 to Sister
      H. Connell." *New York Times*, 29 June 1973, p. 5.

582. "William Inge Must be Spinning in His Grave...."
      Chicago Tribune, 24 July 1979, sec. 2, p. 9.

583. Williams, Tennessee. "Homage." *New York Times*, 1 July
      1973, p. 1.

III
Critical Articles and Reviews of Inge's Work

GENERAL

Articles

584. Armato, Philip M. "The Bum as Scapegoat in William Inge's
Picnic." *Western American Literature* 10 (Winter 1976):
273-282.
Asserts that aside "from being a trenchant analysis
of the pitfalls of interpersonal relationships, *Picnic*
is one of the American theatre's most intelligent in-
vestigations of small town aggression."

585. Balch, Jack. "Anatomy of a Failure." *Theatre Arts*,
February 1960, pp. 10-13.

586. Baxandall, Lee. "Theatre and Affliction." *Encore*, May-
June 1963, pp. 8-13.

587. Brustein, Robert. "The Men-Taming Women of William Inge."
Harper's Magazine, November 1958, pp. 52-57. Also in
The Modern American Theatre, pp. 70-79. Edited by Alvin
B. Kernan. Englewood Cliffs, New Jersey: Prentice-Hall,
1967; and in *Seasons of Discontent*, pp. 83-93. New
York: Simon and Schuster, 1965.
A negative view of Inge as a writer, contending that
he was "yet another example of Broadway's reluctance or
inability to deal intelligently with the American world
at large."

* Burgess, Charles E. "An American Experience: William Inge
in St. Louis, 1943-1949." *Pennsylvania Language and
Literature* 12 (Fall 1976): 438-469. Cited above as
item 536.

588. Christian, George. "A Chat with Inge." *Houston Post*,
1 October 1961, p. 30.

49

589. Clurman, Harold. "Theatre." *Nation*, 7 March 1953,
         pp. 212-213.

590. ————. "William Inge." In *Lies Like Truth: Theatre
         Reviews and Essays*. New York: Macmillan, 1958, pp.
         59-62.

*   "Concerning Labels: 'Most Promising Playwright' Discusses
         Handicaps Imposed by Designation." *New York Times*,
         23 July 1950, sec. 2, p. 1. Cited above as item 98.

591. Driver, Tom F. "Psychologism: Roadblock to Religious
         Drama." *Religion in Life*, Winter 1959-1960, pp. 107-109.

592. Eichelbaum, Stanley. "William Inge's Writing Credo."
         San Francisco Examiner, 31 August 1961, p. 25.

593. Goldstein, Malcolm. "Body and Soul on Broadway." *Modern
         Drama*, February 1965, pp. 411-421.

594. Hamblet, Edwin J. "The North American Outlook of Marcel
         Dubé and William Inge." *Queen's Quarterly* 77 (1970):
         374-387.

595. Hewes, Henry. "Drama." *Saturday Review*, 14 March 1953,
         pp. 15-16, 61.

596. Herron, I.H. "Our Vanishing Towns: Modern Broadway
         Versions." *Southwest Review* 51 (1966): 209-220.

*   Inge, William. "How Do You Like Your Chopin?" *New York
         Times*, 27 February 1955, sec. 2, p. 3. Cited above as
         item 100.

597. Keating, John. "A Bridge for Younger Playwrights."
         Theatre Arts, July 1960, p. 18.

598. Kerr, Walter. "Albee, Miller, Williams: The Sound of
         Self-Parody." In *Thirty Plays Hath September: Pain and
         Pleasure in the Contemporary Theatre*. New York: Simon
         and Schuster, 1969, pp. 220-224.

599. Lambert, J.W. Criticism of *Bus Stop* by William Inge.
         Drama, Summer 1976, pp. 56-58.

600. Lawson, John Howard. "Modern United States Dramaturgy."
         Inostrannaya Literatura 1 (January 1962): 186-196.

* Lewis, Allan. "The Emergent Deans--Kingsley, Inge, and Company." In *American Plays and Playwrights of the Contemporary Theatre*. New York: Crown Publishing, 1965, pp. 143-163. Cited above as item 548.

* Manley, Frances. "William Inge: A Bibliography." *American Book Collector* 16 (October 1965): 13-21. Cited above as item 551.

601. Mitchell, Marilyn. "Teacher as Outsider in the Works of William Inge." *Midwest Quarterly* 17 (July 1976): 385-393.
    Contends that Inge's "opinion of teaching, as of teachers, was ambiguous; he had great respect for it, yet he thought it a profession of those who do not create."

* "More on the Playwright's Mission." *Theatre Arts*, August 1958, p. 19. Cited above as item 102.

602. "Most Promising Playwright." *New York Times*, 23 July 1950, sec. 2, p. 1.

603. "The Playwright, His Mission." United States Information Service, 1956.

604. Seligman, Daniel. "Who Makes Money on Broadway?" *Fortune*, May 1960, pp. 166-169, 288-303.

* "Theatre USA." *Theatre Arts*, October 1958, p. 54. Cited above as item 569.

* Weales, Gerald C. "The New Pineros." In *American Drama Since World War II*. New York: Harcourt, Brace and World, 1962 (item 618), pp. 40-56.

* Williams, Tennessee. "The Writing is Honest." In *The Passionate Playgoer*, pp. 246-249. Edited by George Oppenheimer. New York: Viking Press, 1958. Also in *The Dark at the Top of the Stairs*, pp. vii-ix. By William Inge. New York: Random House, 1958. Cited above as item 574.

605. Wolfson, Lester M. "Inge, O'Neill and the Human Condition." *Southern Speech Journal* 22 (Summer 1957): 221-232.

Books

606. Broussard, Louis. *American Drama: Contemporary Allegory
      from Eugene O'Neill to Tennessee Williams.* Norman:
      University of Oklahoma Press, 1962.

607. Gassner, John. *The Theatre in Our Times.* New York:
      Crown Publishers, Inc., 1954.

608. Gould, Jean. *Modern American Playwrights.* New York:
      Dodd, Mead and Company, 1966.

609. Hewitt, Barnard. *Theatre U.S.A., 1668-1957.* New York:
      McGraw-Hill Book Company, 1959.

610. Jones, Margo. *Theatre-in-the-Round.* New York: Rinehart
      and Company, Inc., 1951.

611. Kerr, Walter. *The Theatre in Spite of Itself.* New York:
      Simon and Schuster, 1963.

612. Lawson, John Howard. *Theory and Techniques of Playwritin(
      New York: Hill and Wang, 1960.

*   Lumley, Frederick. "William Inge." In *New Trends in 20tl
      Century Drama: A Survey Since Ibsen and Shaw.* New York:
      Oxford University Press, 1967, pp. 329-331. Cited
      above as item 549.

613. Macgowan, Kenneth, and Melnitz, William. *The Living
      Stage.* Englewood Cliffs, New Jersey: Prentice-Hall,
      Inc., 1955.

614. Nathan, George Jean. "*Come Back, Little Sheba.*" In
      The Theatre Book of the Year, 1949-1950. New York:
      Alfred A. Knopf, 1950, pp. 232-236.

*   ————. "William Inge." In *The Theatre in the Fifties.*
      New York: Alfred A. Knopf, 1953, pp. 71-76. Cited
      above as item 558.

615. Newquist, Roy. *Counterpoint.* New York: Simon and
      Schuster, 1964, pp. 356-363.

616. Sievers, W. David. *Freud on Broadway.* New York:
      Hermitage House, 1955.

617. Thorp, Willard. *American Writing in the Twentieth Century*. Cambridge: Harvard University Press, 1970.

618. Weales, Gerald C. *American Drama Since World War II*. New York: Harcourt, Brace and World, Inc., 1962.

REVIEWS OF INGE'S PLAYS

Come Back, Little Sheba

First presented by The Theatre Guild at the Booth Theatre, New York City, on February 15, 1950, with the following cast:

(in order of appearance)

Doc	Sidney Blackmer
Marie	Joan Lorring
Lola	Shirley Booth
Turk	Lonny Chapman
Postman	Daniel Reed
Mrs. Coffman	Olga Fabian
Milkman	John Randolph
Messenger	Arnold Schulman
Bruce	Robert Cunningham
Ed Anderson	Wilson Brooks
Elmo Huston	Paul Krauss

Directed by Daniel Mann; Setting and Lighting Designed by Howard Bay; Costumes by Lucille Little; Production under the Supervision of Lawrence Langner and Theresa Helburn; Associate Producer, Phyllis Anderson.

619. Anderson, Phyllis. "Diary of a Production." *Theatre Arts*, November 1950, pp. 58-59.
      Traces the development of *Come Back, Little Sheba* from its earliest written versions through actual production.

620. Atkinson, Brooks. "Two Actors." *New York Times*, 26 February 1950, sec. 2, p. 1.
      Describes the play as a not "wholly satisfactory drama" and says it is "underwritten to the point of barrenness."

621. Beyer, W.H. "The State of the Theatre: Dance, Stage, and 'Drama-Goes-Round.'" *School and Society*, 3 June 1950, pp. 342-346.
      Discusses Inge's underwriting of play.

622. Bolton, Whitney. "Blackmer and Booth Make 'Little Sheba' Noteworthy." *New York Morning Telegraph*, 17 February 1950, p. 6.

623. Clurman, Harold. "A Good Play." *New Republic*, 13 March 1950, pp. 22-23.
      Fits the play to his definition of a "good play."

*   ————. "William Inge." In *Lies Like Truth: Theatre Reviews and Essays*. New York: Macmillan, 1958 (item 590), pp. 59-60.

624. Dusenbury, Winifred Loesch. "Personal Failure." In *The Theme of Loneliness in Modern American Drama*. Gainesville, Florida: University of Florida Press, 1960, pp. 8-37.
      Discusses play as a study of "a woman's loneliness because of her personal failure."

625. Gibbs, Wolcott. "The Dream and the Dog." *New Yorker*, 25 February 1950, pp. 68, 70.
      Describes play as a "peculiar mixture of effective realism and psychological claptrap."

626. Maney, Richard. "Blackmer's Big Scene." *New York Times*, 2 April 1950, sec. 2, p. 3.
      Discusses the pressure on Sidney Blackmer as Doc in the long drunken scene.

*   Nathan, George Jean. "Come Back, Little Sheba." In *The Theatre Book of the Year, 1949-1950*. New York: Alfred A. Knopf, 1950, pp. 232-236. Cited above as item 614.

627. "New Play." *Newsweek*, 27 February 1950, p. 74.
      Favorable review of Inge's "sincerity and skillful writing."

628. "New Play in Manhattan." *Time*, 27 February 1950, p. 81.
      Accuses Inge of tending to "substitute mere sympathy for insight."

629. Nordell, Rod. *Christian Science Monitor*, 25 February
         1950, pp. 22-23.

630. Phelan, Kappo. "The State." *Commonweal*, 3 March 1950,
         p. 558.

631. Watts, Richard, Jr. "The Man, the Dog, and the Bottle."
         New York Post, 16 February 1950, p. 7.

632. Wyatt, Euphemia Van Renssalaer. *Catholic World*, April
         1950, p. 67.

633. Zolotow, Sam. "'Other One' Role to Shirley Booth."
         New York Times, 26 November 1959, p. 57.

Other Reviews

634. *Life*, 17 April 1950, pp. 93+.

635. *New York Theatre Critics' Reviews*, 1950, p. 348.

636. *New York Times*, 16 February 1950, p. 28.

637. *New York Times*, 23 July 1950, sec. 2, p. 1.

638. *Theatre Arts*, April 1950, p. 20.

639. *Theatre Arts*, May 1950, pp. 22-23.

Picnic

Produced by The Theatre Guild and Joshua Logan at
the Music Box Theatre, New York City, on February
19, 1953, with the following cast:

Helen Potts	Ruth McDevitt
Hal Carter	Ralph Meeker
Millie Owens	Kim Stanley
Bomber	Morris Miller
Madge Owens	Janice Rule
Flo Owens	Peggy Conklin
Rosemary Sydney	Eileen Heckart
Alan Seymour	Paul Newman
Irma Kronkite	Reta Shaw
Christine Schoenwalder	Elizabeth Wilson
Howard Bevans	Arthur O'Connell

Directed by Joshua Logan; Scenery and Lighting by
Jo Mielziner.

640.   Atkinson, Brooks. "Inge's Picnic." *New York Times*,
        1 March 1953, sec. 2, p. 1.
            Favorably describes the play as "terse and pertinent."

641.   Barko, Naomi. "William Inge Talks about *Picnic*." *Theatre
        Arts*, July 1953, pp. 66-67.
            Quotes Inge as saying theme of play is that "love
        requires humility."

642.   Bentley, Eric Russell. "Pathetic Phallus." In *Dramatic
        Event: An American Chronicle*. New York: Horizon Press,
        1954, pp. 102-106.

643.   ———. "Pity the Dumb Ox." *New Republic*, 16 March
        1953, pp. 22-23.
            Play "may prove an equally effective piece of
        synthetic folk lore."

644.   Bolton, Whitney. "Inge Does it Again with *Picnic*."
        New York Morning Telegraph, 2 February 1953, p. 8.

645.   Cane, Gigi. "*Picnic*: L'assalto a una fortezza." *Il
        Drama* 231 (December 1955): 11-12.

646.   Clurman, Harold. "Theatre." *Nation*, 7 March 1953,
        pp. 212-213.

*   ———. "William Inge." In *Lies Like Truth: Theatre
        Reviews and Essays*. New York: The Macmillan Company,
        1958 (item 590), pp. 60-62.

647.   Gibbs, Wolcott. "Something Old, Something New." *New
        Yorker*, 28 February 1953, pp. 65-66.
            Describes play as "an interesting and unusual piece,
        full of accurately observed detail."

648.   Hayes, Richard. "The State." *Commonweal*, 20 March 1953,
        p. 603.

649.   Hewes, Henry. *Saturday Review*, 7 March 1953, pp. 33-34.

*   Inge, William. "*Picnic*: From 'Front Porch' to Broadway."
        Theatre Arts, April 1954, pp. 32-33. Cited above as
        item 105.
            Inge describes play as one that should "be enjoyed not
        for the hope of its destination but for what one sees
        along the way."

*   ————. "*Picnic*: Of Women; Variety of Feminine
     Types in a Small Town Will be Seen in a New Play."
     New York Times, 15 February 1953, sec. 2, p. 3. Cited
     above as item 106.

650. Kerr, Walter. *New York Theatre Critics' Reviews*, 1953,
     p. 350. Also in *Theatre U.S.A., 1668-1957* by Barnard
     Hewitt. New York: McGraw-Hill Book Company, 1959,
     pp. 459-461.

651. Lewis, Theophilus. "Theatre." *America*, 2 May 1953,
     p. 147.
         Discusses dismay at Inge's winning of New York Drama
     Critics' Award for play.

652. ————. "Theatre." *America*, 7 March 1953, pp. 632-633.

653. Lundstrom, J.W. "Treachery Afoot." *New York Times*,
     12 April 1953, sec. 2, p. 3.

654. Nathan, George Jean. "Director's Picnic." *Theatre Arts*,
     May 1953, pp. 14-15.
         Mixed review that describes play as a "big Broadway
     show at the expense of a small but doubtless consider-
     ably superior play."

655. "New Play in Manhattan." *Time*, 2 March 1953, pp. 72, 74.
         Play described as "a kind of naturalistic round dance
     of women."

656. "*Picnic* and More Fun." *Saturday Review*, 7 March 1953,
     pp. 33-34.
         Describes play as one which "celebrates the courage
     with which his characters accept the mistakes they must
     substitute for life."

657. "*Picnic* is Chosen Best Native Play." *New York Times*,
     15 April 1953, p. 40.

658. "*Picnic* Tells Conquest of a Kansas Casanova." *Life*,
     16 March 1953, pp. 136-137.

659. "*Picnic*'s Provider." *New Yorker*, 4 April 1953, pp. 24-25.

660. Pyle, John. "Not a Play." *New York Times*, 26 April 1953,
     sec. 2, p. 3.

661. "Reviews." *Newsweek*, 2 March 1953, p. 84.
         Favorable review that applauds Inge because he knows
         how to bring his characters "to life for the theatre."

662. Sheaffer, Louis. "*Picnic*, Fine, Honest Play by Inge of
         Smalltown Life." *Brooklyn Eagle*, 20 February 1953.
         Described as "perceptive, compelling theater."

*   Shuman, R. Baird. *William Inge*. Twayne's United States
         Authors Series, No. 95. New York: Twayne Publishers,
         Inc., 1965 (item 565), pp. 48-56.

*   Sievers, W. David. *Freud on Broadway*. New York: Hermitag
         House, 1955 (item 616), pp. 354-356.

663. Stanley, Kim. "Kim Stanley Talks About *Picnic*." *New
         York Times*, 3 April 1953, p. 54.
         Discusses play from an actor's viewpoint.

*   Weales, Gerald C. *American Drama Since World War II*.
         New York: Harcourt, Brace and World, Inc., 1962 (item
         618), pp. 41, 43-48.

*   Wolfson, Lester M. "Inge, O'Neill and the Human Condition
         Southern Speech Journal 22 (Summer 1957): 225-226 (item
         605).

Other Reviews

664. *Catholic World*, April 1953, p. 69.
         Inge "has created some characters who are doubly real.

665. *New York Times*, 20 February 1953, p. 14.

666. *New York Times*, 30 August 1953, sec. 2, p. 1.

667. *New York Times*, 27 February 1957, p. 32.

668. *Theatre Arts*, October 1953, pp. 28-29.
         Favorable review that describes "poignance" of play.

669. *Variety*, 25 February 1953.
         Describes play as "an obvious prospect for prize
         honors."

Bus Stop

First presented by Robert Whitehead and Roger L.
Stevens at the Music Box Theatre, New York City,
on March 2, 1955, with the following cast:

Elma Duckworth	Phyllis Love
Grace	Elaine Stritch
Will Masters	Lou Polan
Cherie	Kim Stanley
Dr. Gerald Lyman	Anthony Ross
Carl	Patrick McVey
Virgil Blessing	Crahan Denton
Bo Decker	Albert Salmi

Directed by Harold Clurman; Setting by Boris Aron-
son; Costumes and Lighting by Paul Morrison.

670. Atkinson, Brooks. "Mr. Inge in Top Form." *New York
Times*, 13 March 1955, sec. 2, p. 1.

671. Beaufort, John. "'*Bus Stop*,' Ibsen, and 'Silk Stockings.'"
Christian Science Monitor, 12 March 1955.

672. "Best Comedy of the Season." *Life*, 28 March 1955, pp.
77-80.

673. "*Bus Stop* Halt Asked." *New York Times*, 18 July 1956,
p. 22.

674. "*Bus Stop* Suit Settled." *New York Times*, 8 August 1956,
p. 29.

675. Dash, Thomas R. "'*Bus Stop*.'" *Women's Wear Daily*,
3 March 1955.

676. Field, Rowland. "Inge's '*Bus Stop*' Dramatic Delight."
Newark Evening News, 3 March 1955.

677. Gibbs, Wolcott. "Inge, Ibsen, and Some Bright Children."
New Yorker, 12 March 1955, pp. 62, 64, 66-68.
Lauds simplicity of design in play and the "clean
competence of execution."

678. Hatch, Robert. "Theatre." *Nation*, 19 March 1955,
pp. 245-246.
Applauds play as "funny and witty and shrewd."

679. Hayes, Richard. "The Stage." *Commonweal*, 8 April 1955, p. 14.

680. Hewes, Henry. "Mr. Inge's Meringueless Pie." *Saturday Review*, 19 March 1955, p. 24.
        Acclaims play as "the most warmhearted and natural theatre-piece of the season."

681. Lewis, Theophilus. *America*, 9 April 1955, p. 54.

682. "Love at a *Bus Stop*." *New York Times Magazine*, 20 March 1955, p. 59.

683. "New Play in Manhattan." *Time*, 14 March 1955, p. 58.
        Sees play as "the season's and possibly the author's best play."

684. "On Broadway." *Newsweek*, 12 March 1955, p. 99.
        Mixed review that claims Inge "fiddles for the fun of it."

*   Shuman, R. Baird. *William Inge*. Twayne's United States Authors Series, no. 95. New York: Twayne Publishers, Inc., 1965 (item 565), pp. 58-70.

*   Weales, Gerald. *American Drama Since World War II*. New York: Harcourt, Brace and World, Inc., 1962 (item 618), pp. 41, 43-46, 48.

*   Wolfson, Lester M. "Inge, O'Neill and the Human Condition." *Southern Speech Journal* 22 (Summer 1957): 226-227 (item 605).

685. Zolotow, Maurice. "The Season on and off Broadway." *Theatre Arts*, May 1955, pp. 21-22, 86-88.
        Applauds Inge's characterization of play and describes it as a "most enjoyable evening of dramatic pleasure."

Other Reviews

686. *America*, 19 April 1955, p. 54.

687. *Catholic World*, May 1955, p. 147.
        Inge writes "with a smile, which gives charm to the script."

688. *New Republic*, 2 May 1955, p. 22.
        Mixed review that claims Inge harps on "sex sex sex."

689. *New York Times*, 27 February 1955, sec. 2, p. 3.

690. *New York Times*, 3 March 1955, p. 23.

691. *New York Times*, 3 April 1955, sec. 2, p. 1.

692. Deleted.

693. *Variety*, 9 March 1955.
        "Inge has come through with his best script thus
        far."

                    The Dark at the Top of the Stairs

First presented by Saint Subber and Elia Kazan at
the Music Box Theatre, New York City, on December
5, 1957, with the following cast:

Cora Flood	Teresa Wright
Rubin Flood	Pat Hingle
Sonny Flood	Charles Saari
Boy Outside	Jonathan Shawn
Reenie Flood	Judith Robinson
Flirt Conroy	Evans Evans
Morris Lacey	Frank Overton
Lottie Lacey	Eileen Heckart
Punky Givens	Carl Reindel
Sammy Goldenbaum	Timmy Everett
Chauffeur	Anthony Ray

Directed by Elia Kazan; Setting by Ben Edwards;
Costumes by Lucinda Ballard; Lighting by Jean
Rosenthal.

694. Barbour, Thomas. *Commonweal*, 14 March 1958, p. 616.

695. Bolton, Whitney. "'At Top of Stairs' is Inge at His
        Best." *New York Morning Telegraph*, 7 December 1957.

*   Brustein, Robert. "The Men-Taming Women of William
        Inge: *The Dark at the Top of the Stairs*." *Harper's
        Magazine*, November 1958, pp. 52-57. Cited above as
        item 587.

696. Clurman, Harold. "Theatre." *Nation*, 21 December 1957,
         pp. 483-484.
            Describes play as "at once the slightest and the most
         complete" of Inge's works.

697. "[*Dark at the Top of the Stairs* is a play] Culled from
         an Author's Past." *New York Times*, 1 December 1957,
         sec. 2, pp. 1, 3.

698. "*The Dark at the Top of the Stairs*." *Theatre Arts*,
         February 1958, pp. 20-21.

699. Dennis, Patrick. "A Literate Soap Opera." *New Republic*,
         30 December 1957, p. 21.
            Describes play as a soap opera, but of the "best
         French-milled quality."

700. Driver, Tom F. "Hearts and Heads." *Christian Century*,
         1 January 1958, pp. 17-18.
            Describes play as Inge's best since *Come Back, Little
         Sheba*.

701. Freedley, George. *New York Morning Telegraph*, 14 December
         1957.

702. Gassner, John. "Low Men on a Totem Pole: William Inge and
         the Subtragic Muse: *The Dark at the Top of the Stairs*."
         Theatre at the Crossroads. New York: Holt, 1960,
         pp. 167-173.

703. Gibbs, Wolcott. "The Crowded Stairway." *New Yorker*,
         14 December 1957, pp. 83-85.
            Applauds Inge's controlled style and says that play
         is "well worth seeing."

704. Hayes, Richard. "Question of Reality." *Commonweal*,
         14 March 1958, pp. 615-616.
            Describes play as "full of the pleasure of recogni-
         tion."

705. Hewes, Henry. "Light in the Living Room." *Saturday
         Review*, 21 December 1957, p. 27.

706. Kaye, Joseph. "Another Hit by Inge." *Kansas City Star*,
         15 December 1957, p. 11.

707. "New Play in Manhattan." *Time*, 16 December 1957, pp. 42,
     44.
       "With apt and expressive detail, Inge has set his
     scene and animated it."

708. "New Plays." *Educational Theatre Journal*, March 1957,
     p. 81.

*   Shuman, R. Baird. *William Inge*. Twayne's United States
     Authors Series, no. 95. New York: Twayne Publishers,
     Inc., 1965 (item 565), pp. 70-85.

*   Weales, Gerald. *American Drama Since World War II*.
     New York: Harcourt, Brace and World, 1962 (item 618),
     pp. 41-48, 49, 56, 187.

*   Williams, Tennessee. "The Writing is Honest." In *The
     Dark at the Top of the Stairs*. By William Inge. New
     York: Random House, 1953, pp. vii-ix. Cited above as
     item 574.
       Discusses first meeting with Inge in St. Louis and
     the deep respect which he came to have for him.

709. "The World of William Inge." *Theatre Arts*, July 1958,
     pp. 62-64.
       Basically a review of the film version. Comments
     favorably on wide emotional range of Inge's work.

Other Reviews

710. *America*, 11 January 1958, p. 436.

711. *Catholic World*, February 1958, p. 386.
       Favorably says that Inge "has never written so well."

712. *Life*, 6 January 1958, pp. 74-77.

713. *New York Theatre Critics' Reviews*, 1957, p. 158.

714. *New York Times*, 6 December 1957, p. 38.

715. *New York Times*, 15 December 1957, sec. 2, p. 3.

716. *New York Times*, 16 March 1958, sec. 2, p. 1.

717. *New York Times Magazine*, 24 November 1957, pp. 80-81.

718. *Newsweek*, 16 December 1957, p. 81.

719. *Reporter*, 26 December 1957, p. 34.

720. *Saturday Review*, 21 December 1957, pp. 20-21.
         Favorably describes play as "thoughtful" and with
      "humorous insight."

721. *Variety*, 11 December 1957.

                       A Loss of Roses

      First presented by Saint Subber and Lester Oster-
      man at the Eugene O'Neill Theatre, New York City,
      on November 28, 1959, with the following cast:

      Helen Baird   Betty Field
      Kenny   Warren Beatty
      Geoffrey Beamis   Michael J. Pollard
      Lila Green   Carol Haney
      Ronny Cavendish   James O'Rear
      Olga St. Valentine   Margaret Braidwood
      Ricky Powers   Robert Webber
      Mrs. Mulvaney   Joan Morgan

      Staged by Daniel Mann; Setting by Boris Aronson;
      Costumes by Lucinda Ballard; Lighting by Abe Feder.

722. Atkinson, Brooks. "Theatre." *New York Times*, 30 Novem-
         ber 1959.

*   Balch, Jack. "Anatomy of a Failure." *Theatre Arts*,
         February 1960, pp. 10-13. Cited above as item 585.
            Discusses failure of play from standpoint of Inge's
         biographical background.

723. Bolton, Whitney. "Inge Breaks Streak with 'Loss of
         Roses.'" *New York Morning Telegraph*, 1 December 1959.

724. Brustein, Robert. "No Loss: *A Loss of Roses* by William
         Inge and *Natural Affection* by William Inge." In
         Seasons of Discontent: Dramatic Opinions, 1951-1965.
         New York: Simon & Schuster, 1965, pp. 97-101.

725. ————. *New Republic*, 21 December 1959, pp. 23-24.

726. Dash, Thomas R. "*A Loss of Roses* Far, Far from an Inge
         Masterpiece." *Women's Wear Daily*, 30 November 1959.

727. Field, Rowland. "Latest Inge Drama Short of Expectations
         Newark Evening News, 30 November 1959.

728. Haves. "Only Connect...." *Commonweal*, 2 January 1960,
     p. 395.
         Describes play as a "muddled private pathology."

729. Hewes, Henry. "Oedipus Wrecks." *Saturday Review*,
     19 December 1959, p. 24.
         Describes Inge's characters as uninteresting.

730. Kerr, Walter. "First Night Report." *New York Herald
     Tribune*, 30 November 1959.

*   ————. "Mr. Inge." In *The Theatre in Spite of Itself*.
     New York: Simon & Schuster, 1963 (item 611), pp. 238-242.
     Also discusses *The Dark at the Top of the Stairs*.

731. McClain, John. "Inge Wilts in His Latest." *New York
     Journal-American*, 30 November 1959.

732. Tynan, Kenneth. "*A Loss of Roses* by William Inge, at
     the Eugene O'Neill." In *Curtains*. New York: Atheneum,
     1961, pp. 333-335.

733. ————. "Roses and Thorns." *New Yorker*, 12 December
     1959, pp. 99-100.
         An unfavorable review that describes play as fragmentary
     and as a "ritual drama."

734. Watts, Richard, Jr. "Everything Didn't Come Up Roses."
     New York Post, 30 November 1959.

Other Reviews

735. *America*, 2 January 1960, pp. 402+.

736. *Christian Century*, 6 January 1960, p. 15.

737. *Nation*, 19 December 1959, p. 475.

738. *New York Theatre Critics' Reviews*, 1959, p. 211.

739. *New York Times*, 22 November 1959, sec. 2, p. 3.

740. *New York Times*, 30 November 1959, p. 27.

741. *New York Times*, 6 December 1959, sec. 2, p. 5.

742. *New Yorker*, 12 December 1959, p. 24.

743.   *Newsweek*, 7 December 1959, p. 96.

744.   *Theatre Arts*, February 1959, pp. 10-13.

745.   *Time*, 7 December 1959, p. 56.

746.   *Variety*, 2 December 1959.

Natural Affection

First presented by Oliver Smith in association
with Manuel Seff at the Booth Theatre, New York
City, on January 31, 1963, with the following
cast:

Sue Barker	Kim Stanley
Bernie Slovenk	Harry Guardino
Vince Brinkman	Tom Bosley
Claire Brinkman	Monica May
Donnie Barker	Gregory Rozakis
Gil	John Horn
Superintendent	Robert Baines
Sal	Bonnie Bartlett
Max	Gerald Covell

Directed by Tony Richardson; Costumes by Ann Roth;
Lighting by Jack Brown; Music by John Lewis.

747.   Bolton, Whitney. "*Natural Affection* Startlingly Candid."
       New York Morning Telegraph, 2 February 1963.

*   Brustein, Robert. "*Natural Affection* by William Inge."
       In *Seasons of Discontent: Dramatic Opinions, 1951-1965*.
       New York: Simon & Schuster, 1965 (item 724), pp. 100-101

748.   Gassner, John. *Educational Theatre Journal* 15 (May 1963):
       185-186.

749.   McCarten, John. "Tour de Force." *New Yorker*, 9 February
       1963, pp. 66, 68.
          Describes Inge as attempting to become a "junior-
       varsity Tennessee Williams."

750.   "*Natural Affection*." *Theatre Arts*, March 1963, pp. 58-59.

*   Shuman, R. Baird. *William Inge*. Twayne's United States
       Authors Series, no. 95. New York: Twayne Publishers,
       Inc., 1965 (item 565), pp. 109-121.

751. Taubman, Howard. "The Theatre: *Natural Affection*."
      New York Times, 2 February 1963, p. 5.

Other Reviews

752. *Commonweal*, 1 March 1963, p. 598.

753. *Nation*, 16 February 1963, p. 148.

754. *New Republic*, 23 February 1963, p. 29.

755. *New York Theatre Critics' Reviews*, 1963, p. 383.

756. *Newsweek*, 11 February 1963, p. 84.

757. *Reporter*, 25 April 1963, pp. 48-49.

758. *Saturday Review*, 16 February 1963, p. 25.

759. *Time*, 8 February 1963, p. 56.

Where's Daddy?

First presented by Michael Wager by arrangement
with Robert Whitehead at the Billy Rose Theatre,
New York City, on March 2, 1966, with the following cast:

Teena	Barbara Dana
Tom	Beau Bridges
Mrs. Bigelow	Betty Field
Razz	Robert Hooks
Helen	Barbara Ann Teer
Pinky	Hiram Sherman

Directed by Harold Clurman; Setting and Lighting
by Ben Edwards; Clothes by Jane Greenwood.

Other Reviews

760. *Commonweal*, 8 April 1966, p. 83.

761. *New Republic*, 26 March 1966, p. 36.

762. *New York Theatre Critics' Reviews*, 1966, p. 347.

763. *New York Times*, 3 March 1966, p. 27.

764. *New Yorker*, 12 March 1966, p. 110.

765. *Newsweek*, 14 March 1966, p. 94.

766. *Saturday Review*, 19 March 1966, p. 55.

767. *Time*, 11 March 1966, p. 52.

768. *Vogue*, 5 April 1966, p. 64.

Summer Brave

Presented Friday, October 24, 1975, by Barry M.
Brown, Burry Fredrik, Fritz Holt and Sally Sears
in association with Robert Straus as a part of
the Kennedy Center and Xerox Corporation American
Bicentennial Theatre Production at the ANTA
Theatre in New York City, with the following cast:

Alexis Smith
Nan Martin
Ernest Thompson
Jill Eikenberry
Joe Ponazecki
Peter Weller
Sheila Adams
Alice Drummond
Martha Greenhouse
Patricia O'Connell

Directed by Michael Montel; Scenery by Stuart Wurt-
zel; Lighting by David Segal (originally produced
for the Kennedy Center by Roger L. Stevens and
Richmond Crinkley).

NOTE: *Summer Brave* was a new version of *Picnic*.

769. "Broadway Back in Brisk Box Office Stride; 'Treemonisha'
Strong at $112,666." *Variety*, 29 October 1975, p. 70.

770. "Broadway Up; 'Travesties' $76,777; 'Wiz' $134,823,
'Treemonisha' N.G." *Variety*, 12 November 1975, p. 64.
Announces early close of *Summer Brave* after second
week (original four-week run planned) at a loss of
about $175,000.

771. "Late Bill Inge's *Summer Brave* Ties to *Picnic*."
Variety, 4 July 1973, p. 57.

772.   [Review of *Summer Brave*].   *New York Times*, 2 November
          1975, sec. D, p. 3.

773.   "Rex Reed Salutes *Summer Brave*."   *New York Times*,
          2 November 1975, sec. D, p. 3.
             Advertisement--review originally printed in *Sunday
          News*.

REVIEWS OF INGE'S NOVELS

Good Luck, Miss Wyckoff

Reviews 1970

774.   *Best Sellers*, 1 June 1970, p. 91.

775.   *Book List*, 15 July 1970, p. 1381.

776.   *Book World*, 14 June 1970, p. 8.

777.   *Kirkus Reviews*, 15 March 1970, p. 345.

778.   *Kirkus Reviews*, 1 April 1970.

779.   *Library Journal*, 1 May 1970, p. 1760.

780.   *Life*, 22 May 1970, p. 12.

781.   *National Observer*, 27 July 1970, p. 17.

782.   *New York Times Book Review*, 14 June 1970, p. 24.

783.   *Publishers Weekly*, 16 March 1970, p. 54.

784.   *Saturday Review*, 27 June 1970, p. 35.

785.   *Southwest Review*, Fall 1970, p. 426.

786.   *Virginia Quarterly Review*, Summer 1970, p. R88.

787.   *Wall Street Journal*, 13 July 1970, p. 10.

Reviews 1971

788. *Book World*, 26 March 1971, p. 9.

789. *Catholic World*, March 1971, p. 328.

790. *New Statesman*, 26 March 1971, p. 434.

791. *Observer*, 28 March 1971, p. 32.

792. *Publishers Weekly*, 22 March 1971, p. 54.

793. *Spectator*, 3 April 1971, p. 459.

My Son is a Splendid Driver

Reviews 1971

794. *Best Sellers*, 15 June 1971, p. 132.

795. *Book List*, 1 September 1971, p. 36.

796. *Christian Science Monitor*, 8 July 1971, p. 11.

797. *Kirkus Reviews*, 1 April 1971, p. 393.

798. *Kirkus Reviews*, 15 April 1971, p. 454.

799. *Library Journal*, 1 May 1971, p. 1636.

800. *National Review*, 29 June 1971, p. 708.

801. *New Reviews*, 3 July 1971, p. 30.

802. *Publishers Weekly*, 19 April 1971, p. 44.

THESES AND DISSERTATIONS
ABOUT INGE'S WORKS

803. Barrett, Charles M. "William Inge, The Mid-Century
      Playwright." Master of Arts thesis in Drama, Univer-
      sity of North Carolina at Chapel Hill, 1957.

804. Bottje, Wayne D. "A Study of Six Representative American Post World War II Playwrights." Master's thesis, Kansas State College of Pittsburg, 1965.

805. Brucel, Joseph Francis. "The Theme of Loneliness in the Major Plays of William Inge." Master's thesis, Michigan State University, 1955.

806. Clarkson, Philip Bayard. "The Evolution from Conception to Production of the Dramas of William Inge." Ph.D. dissertation, Stanford University, 1963. [See *Dissertation Abstracts*, 24 (1963): 1285. Order No. 63-6420.]

807. Crawford, Jerry Leroy. "An Analysis of the Dramatic Structure in Three Plays by William Inge." Master's thesis, Stanford University, 1957.

808. Gobrecht, Elenor Alverta. "A Descriptive Study of the Value Commitments of the Principal Characters in Four Recent American Plays: *Picnic*, *Cat on a Hot Tin Roof*, *Long Day's Journey into Night*, and *Look Homeward, Angel*." Ph.D. dissertation, University of Southern California, 1963. [See *Dissertation Abstracts*, 24 (1963): 433-434. Order No. 63-4225.]

809. Harvey, Barbara Nell. "The Independence, Kansas, Theatrical Influence on Playwright William Inge." Master's problem, Department of Speech and Theatre, Kansas State College of Pittsburg, 1969.

810. Lockwood, Patton. "The Plays of William Motter Inge, 1948-1960." Ph.D. dissertation, Michigan State University, 1962. [See *Dissertation Abstracts*, 24 (1963): 895. Order No. 63-3731.]

811. Reeves, Adrienne Ellis. "The Dramatization of Female Frustration in Four Plays by William Inge." Master of Arts thesis in Speech and Drama, San José [California] State College, 1960.

IV
William Inge and Film

ADAPTATIONS OF INGE'S WORKS

Come Back, Little Sheba

Wallis Hagen, Inc. Released by Paramount Pictures
Corp. 1953. Black and White. 35 mm. 99 minutes.
With the following cast:

Shirley Booth
Burt Lancaster
Terry Moore
Richard Jaeckel
Philip Ober

Producer, Hal B. Wallis; Director, Daniel Mann;
Screenplay, Ketti Frings; Editor, Warren Low;
Music, Franz Waxman.

812. Anderson, Lindsay. *Sight and Sound*, April-June 1953,
pp. 196-197.

813. Vermilye, Jerry. *Burt Lancaster: A Pictorial History
of His Films*. New York: Falcon, 1971.

Other Reviews

814. *Catholic World*, January 1953, p. 302.
Described as "an unusual motion picture."

815. *Christian Century*, 4 March 1953, p. 271.

816. *Commonweal*, 26 December 1952, p. 308.

817. *Films in Review*, January 1953, pp. 37-38.

818. *Harper's*, January 1953, p. 94.
Inge "never preaches; he avoids banalities; he skirts
sentimentality but is not frightened by sentiment."

819. *Holiday*, February 1953, pp. 22-23.

820. *Library Journal*, 15 January 1953, p. 141.
     Described as "a triumph for Shirley Booth."

821. *McCall's*, February 1953, p. 9.

822. *Nation*, 8 November 1952, p. 434.

823. *National Observer*, 8 November 1952.

824. *New York Times*, 16 November 1952, sec. 4, pp. 58-59.

825. *New York Times*, 14 December 1952, sec. 2, p. 5.

826. *New York Times*, 24 December 1952, p. 13.

827. *New York Times*, 11 January 1953, sec. 2, p. 1.

828. *New Yorker*, 27 December 1952, p. 59.

829. *Newsweek*, 29 December 1952, p. 64.
     Describes film as "one of Hollywood's few outstanding
     movies of the year," and Shirley Booth's Lola as
     "Hollywood's best performance of the year."

830. *Saturday Review*, 27 December 1952, p. 26.
     Asserts "the heart of Inge's play has been translated
     to the screen with rare fidelity."

831. *Theatre Arts*, December 1952, p. 29.
     Concludes that this film "makes the general run of
     movies look like so much celluloid."

832. *Theatre Arts*, February 1953, p. 15.

833. *Time*, 29 December 1952, p. 66.
     Describes film as "a minor but moving tragedy on a
     major theme; the lives of quiet desperation that men
     lead."

Picnic

Columbia Pictures Corporation. 1956. Color. 35
mm. 115 minutes. With the following cast:

William Holden
Rosalind Russell
Kim Novak
Betty Field
Susan Strasberg

Producer, Fred Kohlmar; Director, Joshua Logan;
Screenplay, Daniel Taradash; Editors, Charles
Nelson and William A. Lyon; Music, George Dunning;
Music Conductor, Morris Stoloff; Orchestrations,
Arthur Morton.

834. Mannock, P.L. *Films and Filming*, March 1956, pp. 16-17.

835. Prouse, Derek. *Sight and Sound*, Spring 1956, pp. 194-196.

836. Quirk, Lawrence J. *The Films of William Holden.*
Secaucus, New Jersey: Citadel Press, 1973.

837. Sarris, Andrew. *Film Culture*, 1956, pp. 26-27.

838. Springer, John. *Films in Review*, January 1956, pp. 32-33.

839. Steen, Mike. *Hollywood Speaks: An Oral History.* New
York: Putnam, 1974.

840. Yanni, Nicholas. *Rosalind Russell.* New York: Pyramid
Press, 1975.

Other Reviews

841. *America*, 25 February 1956, p. 600.

842. *Catholic World*, February 1956, pp. 383-384.
Concludes that "the serious-minded filmgoer may find
Picnic an impressive production."

843. *Commonweal*, 2 March 1956, p. 569.

844. *Cosmopolitan*, February 1956, p. 24.

845. *Library Journal*, 15 January 1956, p. 175.
The film version "proves to be superb material for
Technicolor and the wide screen."

846. *Look*, 24 January 1956, pp. 80-82.

847. *Nation*, 25 February 1956, p. 167.

848. *National Parent-Teacher*, February 1956, p. 40.

849. *New York Times*, 7 August 1955, sec. 2, p. 5.

850. *New York Times*, 17 February 1956, p. 13.

851. *New York Times*, 19 February 1956, sec. 2, p. 1.

852. *New York Times Magazine*, 25 December 1955, p. 26.

853. *New Yorker*, 25 February 1956, p. 127.

854. *Newsweek*, 13 February 1956, p. 100.

855. *Saturday Review*, 18 February 1956, p. 25.
     Film is "in many ways a notable movie."

856. *Woman's Home Companion*, March 1956, pp. 32-33.

Bus Stop

Twentieth Century-Fox Film Corporation. 1956.
Color. 35 mm. 96 minutes. With the following
cast:

Marilyn Monroe
Don Murray
Arthur O'Connell
Betty Field
Eileen Heckart

Producer, Buddy Adler; Director, Joshua Logan;
Screenplay, George Axelrod; Editor, William
Reynolds; Music, Alfred Newman and Cyril J. Mock-
ridge; Music Conductor, Alfred Newman.

857. Baker, Peter G. *Films and Filming*, November 1956, p. 24.

858. Conway, Michael, and Ricci, Mark. *The Films of Marilyn
     Monroe*. New York: Citadel, 1964.

859. Guiles, Fred Lawrence. *Norma Jean: The Life of Marilyn
     Monroe*. New York: McGraw-Hill, 1969.

860. Kobal, John, ed. *Marilyn Monroe: A Life on Film*.
     London and New York: Hamlyn, 1974.

861. Mailer, Norman. *Marilyn: A Biography*. New York: Grosset
     and Dunlap, 1973.

862. Mellen, Joan. *Marilyn Monroe*. New York: Pyramid, 1973.

863. Monroe, Marilyn. *My Story*. New York: Stein and Day,
     1974.

864. Wagenknecht, Edward, ed. *Marilyn Monroe: A Composite View.* Philadelphia: Chilton, 1969.

865. Wood, Eloise. *Films in Review,* October 1956, pp. 413-414.

866. Zolotow, Maurice. *Marilyn Monroe.* New York: Harcourt, Brace, 1960.

Other Reviews

867. *America,* 15 September 1956, p. 576.

868. *Catholic World,* October 1956, p. 66.

869. *Commonweal,* 7 September 1956, p. 561.

870. *Coronet,* August 1956, p. 8.

871. *Library Journal,* 1 October 1956, p. 2174.
        Described as a "thoroughly engaging and entertaining film."

872. *Life,* 27 August 1956, pp. 79-80.

873. *Nation,* 6 October 1956, p. 294.

874. *National Parent-Teacher,* October 1956, p. 37.

875. *New York Times,* 1 September 1956, p. 19.

876. *New York Times,* 2 September 1956, sec. 2, p. 1.

877. *New York Times,* 9 September 1956, sec. 2, p. 1.

878. *New Yorker,* 15 September 1956, p. 76.

879. *Newsweek,* 27 August 1956, p. 90.
        Described as "well worth a ride."

880. *Saturday Review,* 15 September 1956, p. 76.

881. *Theatre Arts,* October 1956, pp. 47-49.

882. *Time,* 3 September 1956, p. 74.
        Described as "neatly paced and satisfying."

The Dark at the Top of the Stairs

Warner Brothers Corporation. 1960. Color. 35
mm. 123 minutes. With the following cast:

Robert Preston
Dorothy McGuire
Shirley Knight
Robert Eyer
Eve Arden
Angela Lansbury
Lee Kinsolving
Frank Overton
Penney Parker
Harry Ralston

Producer, Michael Garrison; Director, Delbert Mann;
Screenplay, Harriet Frank, Jr. and Irving Ravetch.

883.   Cutts, John. *Films and Filming*, November 1960, p. 29.

884.   Hart, Henry. *Films in Review*, October 1960, pp. 485–486.

Other Reviews

885.   *America*, 8 October 1960, p. 56.

886.   *Commonweal*, 14 October 1960, pp. 73–74.

887.   *Filmfacts*, 1960, p. 217.

888.   *New York Times*, 23 September 1960, p. 33.

889.   *New York Times*, 25 September 1960, sec. 2, p. 1.

890.   *New Yorker*, 1 October 1960, p. 167.

891.   *Newsweek*, 26 September 1960, p. 119.

892.   *Saturday Review*, 17 September 1960, p. 44.
       Described as "a film filled with rare insights into
       rarely discussed problems."

893.   *Time*, 12 September 1960, p. 80.
       Reviewer states that "this is Inge country."

The Stripper

Jerry Wald Productions. Distributed by Twentieth
Century-Fox Film Corporation. 1963. Black and
White. 35 mm. 95 minutes. With the following
cast:

Joanne Woodward
Richard Beymer
Claire Trevor
Carol Lynley
Robert Webber
Louis Nye
Gypsy Rose Lee
Michael J. Pollard
Sondra Kerr
Susan Brown
Marlene De Lamater
Gary Pagett
Ralph Lee
Bing Russell

Producer, Jerry Wald; Associate Producer, Curtis
Harrington; Director, Franklin J. Schaffner;
Screenplay, Meade Roberts; Editor, Robert Simpton;
Music, Jerry Goldsmith; Dance Director, Alex
Romero.

NOTE: This is a screen verson of William Inge's
1959 play *A Loss of Roses*.

894. Bean, Robin. *Films and Filming*, June 1963, pp. 28-29.

895. Comerford, Adelaide. *Films in Review*, May 1963, p. 310.

896. Sussex, Elizabeth. *Sight and Sound*, Summer 1963, p. 146.

Other Reviews

897. *Commonweal*, 29 June 1963, p. 377.

898. *Filmfacts*, 1963, p. 118.

899. *New York Times*, 20 June 1963, p. 29.

900. *Saturday Review*, 13 July 1963, p. 16.

901. *Time*, 3 May 1963, p. 109.

Bus Riley's Back in Town

Universal Pictures. 1965. Color. 35 mm. 93
minutes [Copyright length 100 minutes]. With the
following cast:

Ann-Margret
Michael Parks
Janet Margolin
Brad Dexter
Crahan Denton
Jocelyn Brando
Kim Darby
Larry Storch
Mimsey Farmer
Brett Somers
Nan Martin
Lisabeth Hush
Ethel Griffies
Alice Pearce
Chet Stratton
David Carradine
Marc Cavell
Parley Baer

Producer, Elliott Kastner; Director, Harvey Hart;
Assistant Directors, Terence Nelson, Bill Gilmore;
Screenplay, Walter Gage (see note); Director of
Photography, Russell Metty; Editor, Folmar Blang-
sted; Assistant Editor, Monte Hellman; Music,
Richard Markowitz; Choreography, David Winters.

NOTE: Walter Gage is a pseudonym for William Inge,
who requested that his name be removed from the
credits.

902. Eyles, Allen. *Films and Filming*, November 1965, p. 27.

903. Gillett, John. *Sight and Sound*, Winter 1965-1966, p. 43.

904. Hodgens, R.M. *Film Quarterly*, Summer 1965, p. 59.

*   Shuman, R. Baird. *William Inge*. Twayne's United States
      Authors Series, no. 95. New York: Twayne Publishers,
      Inc., 1965. Cited above as item 565.

Other Review

905. *Filmfacts*, 1965, p. 54.

ORIGINAL SCREENPLAY BY INGE

Splendor in the Grass

NBI Productions–Newton Productions. Distributed
by Warner Brothers Pictures. 1961. Color. 35
mm. 124 minutes. With the following cast:

Natalie Wood
Warren Beatty
Pat Hingle
Audrey Christie
Barbara Loden
Zohra Lampert
Fred Stewart
Joanna Roos
Jan Norris

Producer–Director, Elia Kazan; Assistant Director,
Don Kranze; Associate Producers, William Inge,
Charles H. Maguire; Original Story and Screenplay,
William Inge; Editor, Gene Milford; Music Composer
and Conductor, David Amram; Choreographer, George
Tapps.

906. Armitage, Peter. *Film*, Spring 1962, p. 13.

907. Basinger, Jeanine; Frazer, John; and Reed, Joseph W.,
Jr., eds. *Working with Kazan*. Middletown, Connecticut:
Wesleyan University, 1973.

908. Bean, Robin. *Films and Filming*, February 1962, pp. 29–30.

909. Clark, Arthur B. *Films in Review*, November 1961, pp. 555–
556.

910. Hatch, Robert. *Nation*, 4 November 1961, p. 363.

911. Hawkins, Robert F. "Quality and Variety Keynote Annual
Cannes Festival." *New York Times*, 3 June 1962, sec. 2,
p. 5.

912. Hodgens, R.M. *Film Quarterly*, Winter 1961–1962, p. 61.

913. "Inge Sets Limits as Film Scenarist." *New York Times*,
25 August 1961, p. 17.

914. Kempton, Murray. "Natalie Wood: Is *This* the Girl Next
Door?" *Show*, March 1962, pp. 50–53.

915. Knight, Arthur. "It's Controversial." *Saturday Review*,
      16 September 1961, p. 36.
          States that "the combination of detached writing and
      impassioned direction makes it constantly fascinating
      to watch, and its obvious integrity can earn it only
      respect."

916. ————. "Outside Looking In." *Saturday Review*, 5 May
      1962, p. 28.

917. "New Scenarist's Views." *New York Times*, 8 October 1961,
      sec. 2, p. 9.

918. "Personal Creation in Hollywood: Can It Be Done?" A
      discussion by John Houseman, Fred Zinnemann, Irvin
      Kershner, Terry Sanders, Kent Mackenzie, Gavin Lambert,
      and Pauline Kael. *Film Quarterly*, Spring 1962, pp. 16-
      24.

*   Shuman, R. Baird. *William Inge*. Twayne's United States
      Authors Series, no. 95. New York: Twayne Publishers,
      Inc., 1965. Cited above as item 565.

919. Weales, Gerald. "In the Grass, Alas." *Reporter*,
      23 November 1961, pp. 43-44.
          Negative review that contends "the film achieves
      no texture of its own...."

Other Reviews

920. *America*, 14 October 1961, p. 60.

921. *Commonweal*, 27 October 1961, p. 121.

922. *Esquire*, December 1961, p. 66.

923. *Filmfacts*, 1961, p. 239.

924. *New Republic*, 16 October 1961, p. 21.

925. *New York Post*, 11 October 1961.
          Reviewer lauds film and states its "unpretentious
      yet perfect grasp of truth surely places it among the
      best films from anywhere that you can see this year."

926. *New York Times*, 22 May 1960, sec. 2, p. 7.

927. *New York Times*, 30 April 1961, sec. 4, p. 49.

928. *New York Times*, 11 October 1961, p. 53.
          Describes film as "a frank and ferocious social
      drama...."

929. *New York Times*, 15 October 1961, sec. 2, p. 1.

930. *New Yorker*, 14 October 1961, pp. 177-178.
          Reviewer describes the film as "phony."

931. *Newsweek*, 16 October 1961, p. 112.
          "Out of these faulty mortals, Kazan, Inge, and cast
      have created a movie that is funny, moving, and
      finally beautiful."

932. *Time*, 13 October 1961, p. 95.
          A mixed review that describes the film as "slick,
      exciting, professional in every detail...."

SCREEN ADAPTATION BY INGE

All Fall Down

John Houseman Productions. Distributed by Metro-
Goldwyn-Mayer, Inc. 1962. Black and White. 35
mm. 111 minutes. With the following cast:

Eva Marie Saint
Warren Beatty
Karl Malden
Angela Lansbury
Brandon De Wilde
Constance Ford
Barbara Baxley
Evans Evans
Madame Spivy
Jennifer Howard
Albert Paulsen
Henry Kulky
Collette Jackson
Robert Sorrells
Bernadette Withers
Carol Kelly
Paul Bryar

Producer, John Houseman; Associate Producer,
Ethel Winant; Director, John Frankenheimer;
Assistant Director, Hal Polaire; Screenplay,
William Inge (see note); Editor, Frederic Stein-
kamp; Music, Alex North.

NOTE: Screenplay by William Inge is adapted from
the novel by James Leo Herlihy (New York:
Pocket Books, 1961).

933. Bean, Robin. *Films and Filming*, June 1962, p. 38.

934. Beckley, Paul V. "The New Movies." *New York Herald
Tribune*, 12 April 1962.

935. Crowther, Bosley. "The Screen: *All Fall Down*." *New
York Times*, 12 April 1962, p. 41.

936. Filmer, Paul. *Screen*, July–October 1969, pp. 160–173.

937. Fitzpatrick, Ellen. *Films in Review*, May 1962, pp. 297–
298.

938. Speegle, Paul. *San Francisco News Call Bulletin*,
30 March 1962, p. 16.

939. Taylor, John Russell. *Sight and Sound*, Summer 1962,
p. 144.

Other Reviews

940. *America*, 1962, p. 210.

941. *Commonweal*, 27 April 1962, p. 112.

942. *Esquire*, October 1962, p. 28.

943. *Filmfacts*, 1962, p. 71.

944. *New Republic*, 23 April 1962, pp. 37–38.
      The film is described as a "delicate and moving
      transcription" of the novel.

945. *New York Post*, 12 April 1962.
      "This is one of the fine American films of the year
      in its matched qualities of story, place, person, and
      human significance."

946. *New York Times*, 22 April 1962, sec. 2, p. 1.

947. *New Yorker*, 21 April 1962, p. 170.

948. *Newsweek*, 23 April 1962, pp. 96-97.
     A "striking" film that earns Inge praise for his
     adaptation of the novel.

949. *Saturday Review*, 5 May 1962, p. 28.

950. *Time*, 13 April 1962, p. 100.

TELEVISION PLAY BY INGE

Out on the Outskirts of Town

Produced by Dick Berg for Chrysler Theater ("Bob
Hope Presents") on NBC-TV, November 6, 1964, with
the following cast:

Anne Bancroft
Jack Warden
Fay Bainter

Producer, Dick Berg; Original Television Play,
William Inge.

951. Gould, Jack. "TV: Inge's '*Out on the Outskirts of Town*.'"
     New York Times, 7 November 1964, p. 54.
     Bancroft's acting is praised, but the play is called
     a "pedestrian melodrama" with "cliché-ridden dialogue."

INDEX